HEROISM AND THE BLACK INTELLECTUAL

HEROISM

AND THE BLACK INTELLECTUAL

BY JERRY GAFIO WATTS

POLITICS, AND AFRO-AMERICAN INTELLECTUAL LIFE

RALPH ELLISON,

the
university
of north
carolina
press
chapel hill
& london

© 1994 The University
of North Carolina Press
All rights reserved

Manufactured in the United States
of America

The paper in this book meets the
guidelines for permanence and dur-
ability of the Committee on Production Guidelines for Book Longevity
of the Council on Library Resources.

Design by April Leidig-Higgins

Library of Congress
Cataloging-in-Publication Data

Watts, Jerry Gafio.
  Heroism and the black intellectual :
Ralph Ellison, politics, and Afro-
American intellectual life / Jerry
Gafio Watts.
    p. cm.
  Includes bibliographical references
and index.
    ISBN 0-8078-2164-0 (cloth : alk.
paper). — ISBN 0-8078-4477-2
(pbk. : alk. paper)
    1. Ellison, Ralph—Political and
social views. 2. Politics and literature—United States—History—20th
century. 3. Afro-Americans—Politics
and government. 4. Afro-Americans—Intellectual life. 5. Afro-
Americans in literature. 6. Courage in
literature. 7. Heroes in literature.
8. Race in literature.
I. Title.
PS3555.L625Z95   1994   94-5724
818'.5409—dc20   CIP

Permission to reproduce selected
material can be found on p. 157.

98 97 96 95 94 5 4 3 2 1

FOR MARIE AND CHIEF, MY BELOVED PARENTS

Contents

ACKNOWLEDGMENTS

No author is an island. I am no exception. In writing this book I have benefited from the help of many persons. Yet, my intellectual style is exceptionally solitary. Except for those scholars of Ellison who preceded me in print, no single person or group of persons has had an identifiably singular influence on the shape of this work.

These reflections on Ralph Ellison first took form as a long chapter in a very long dissertation. As a student of American politics, I was fortunate to attend graduate school at Yale during the late 1970s. The Yale political science department allowed me, an Americanist, to study something other than public policy analysis or voting behavior tabulations. I would like to thank Stanley Greenberg, Juan Linz, David Apter, James Scott, Doug Rae, Robert Lane, and the late Philip White for their support during my graduate school years. Professor David Apter, my dissertation chairman, deserves special mention.

My interests in Afro-American intellectuals began early in my life. When I was in the first grade, my mother returned to college to complete her B.A. I remember her periodically reciting to the family statements made in class by her sociology professor, E. Franklin Frazier. My father was equally proud of the faculty of Howard University. By the time I was in the fourth grade, I knew about Charles Drew, Benjamin Mays, William Hastie, Frank Snowden, W. Montague Cobb, Rayford Logan, Ralph Bunche, Charles Houston, John Hope Franklin, and other noteworthy past and present faculty of that institution. I had no idea what these men actually contributed to the world, but I knew, for instance, that Rayford Logan had graduated Phi Beta Kappa from Williams and that Hastie had done likewise at Amherst. Looking back, I am amazed that I could recite so many facts about individual Afro-American intellectual achievers and yet understand so little. While I generally believed that achieving Phi Beta Kappa meant that one was smart, I did not understand its significance or, for that matter, the significance of Amherst College. Yet, at this very early moment, I was told by my parents that I too could attend one of those "dream colleges" like Bowdoin or Swarthmore provided that I did well in school. I received good grades in school. My parents kept their promise. In the fall of 1971 I entered Harvard College.

I have been a formal student of Afro-American intellectual life since that day in September 1972 when I first sat down in Martin Kilson's survey course on Afro-American politics. I can no longer recall whether it was Kilson's unique way of thinking or his obtrusive deviancy, rhetorical and sartorial, that first attracted me. In some respects my earlier memories of Kilson are a fog because he was a larger-than-life person to me. During my final three years at Harvard and continuing throughout my initial years of graduate study at Yale, Kilson was a constant source of information and insight into the political behavior of Afro-American intellectuals. More importantly, the time Kilson shared with me as a

Harvard undergraduate helped me to develop certain crucial habits and disciplines of the mind. Whereas my decision to become a professor of political science also owes an immense debt to Martin Kilson's example, the arguments in this book are not in any direct way indebted to him. However, to the extent that I am trying to critically confront in Ellison a sacred icon of the Afro-American intellectual world, my work is decidedly Kilsonian.

At crucial moments in graduate school Eugene Rivers and Frank Gonzales helped me to avoid traps of intellectual parochialism. Eugene helped me to generate grander intellectual ambitions, far beyond those that I brought to graduate school. Frank encouraged my interests in social theory. Jackie Lindsay provided me with my first real images of a healthy, integrated intellectual life.

People who helped to sharpen my grasp of Ellison include Horace Porter, Cornel West, Farah Griffin, James A. Miller, Martin Kilson, and Robert O'Meally. O'Meally deserves special mention for the hours spent in Wesleyan's Center for Afro-American Studies helping a "Wrightman" like myself come to greater appreciation of Ellison and Albert Murray. Additional encouragement and support came from Carla O'Connor, Deborah King, James Watts, Jr., Al Young, Amy Randall, Clarence Walker, Kathy Rees, Alex Dupuy, Paul Lauter, Kris Graves, Paul Kumar, Henry Louis Gates, Marcus Bruce, Dina Anselmi, Erness Brody, Sandy Sydlo, Natalie Difloff, Barbara Sicherman, Roberta Gold, Penny Von Eschen, Carl Jorgensen, David Evans, Emma Ketteringham, Robert Wood, Earl Smith, Gerald Hudson, Fred Montas, MaryAnn Clawson, Robert Watts, Paula West, and numerous others.

A special note of appreciation must go to Werner Sollors, Cornel West, and Horace Porter for their enthusiastic support of this project.

Leon Sigal, a colleague in the Wesleyan government department gave me a wonderful and unanticipated psychic lift by voluntarily editing an earlier draft of this work. His extraordinary generosity will never be forgotten.

Glenna Goulet expertly typed the manuscript in all of its postdissertation revised phases.

This project benefited immensely from faculty research grants provided by the University of California, Davis; Wesleyan University; and Trinity College, Hartford. I also benefited from a Ford Foundation postdoctoral fellowship for minority scholars and a fellowship from the American Council of Learned Societies for recent recipients of the Ph.D. This book is only one installment of my gratitude for the generosity of the above.

Traci C. West, my wife and companion, has been with me throughout the actual writing of this manuscript both in dissertation form and now in this drastically revised state. She has endured. She will not believe that this project has been completed until she holds a copy of the published book. While I appreciate Traci for many things, I am particularly indebted to her for helping me to fight the demon of intellectual insecurity masquerading as intellectual bravado, unrealizable ambitiousness, and hypercompetitiveness. This particular neurosis has made the writing of this book far more difficult and anxiety ridden than it need be. Hopefully, future writing tasks will be less torturous.

Finally, I thank Ralph Ellison for giving me and my generation an intellectual presence and a corpus of work worthy of serious engagement. I hope that my respect for him and his work is evident.

This book was already in press when I heard the news that Ralph Ellison had died. The publishers and I agreed to retain references to Ellison in the present tense rather than to make changes that would delay the appearance of a study that now seeks to honor his memory by fostering serious discussion of his important work.

HEROISM
AND THE BLACK INTELLECTUAL

I tried to strike a conversation. I asked Ellison if he had read my book. He said, "Yes, I bought a copy three weeks ago."

Both of us were in radical movement years ago. He and I understood Negro society as no other writers do. I can read between the lines. He can't get involved in the Negro movement.

The ideological battle is the most bitter and devastating battle there is. Ex-communist turns on Communist. Ellison knows that I know; but he knows I cannot be bought. I haven't changed; he has.

Ten years ago in this room we argued about the individual vs. Socialist. He doesn't know to what extent I may go in joining other writers in attacking him. I have to write an article on Negro writers. Our social approach is different. In H.G. I write about an opulent society serving the Belshazzarian feast. He is an individualist. I am a social writer. Ellison claims he is a descendant of Emerson. He says the Negro endures; I say he advances. He and I have debated long. I don't want to write an Alger story of a Negro who succeeded. I have a social approach to man's problems.—Melvin Tolson

ESCAPING THE GHOST OF HAROLD CRUSE

Students of the political behavior of Afro-American intellectuals are indebted to and burdened by the writings of Harold Cruse. Twenty-five years after its initial publication, *The Crisis of the Negro Intellectual*[1] must by now be considered a classic text in Afro-American cultural studies, for it remains one of the most provocative and suggestive treatments of the political behavior and beliefs of twentieth-century Afro-American intellectuals. Cruse's importance lay in his ability to discuss perceptively and to situate historically some of the major political and aesthetic controversies woven throughout the very marrow of the twentieth-century, Afro-American intellectual enterprise. Published during the late 1960s, *The Crisis of the Negro Intellectual* became the coalescing spark for highly contentious intellectual exchanges within the Afro-American intelligentsia. Many of these debates centered around questions relating to the responsibility of the black intellectual. Yet, the very qualities that made *The Crisis of the Negro Intellectual* such a controversial text are the same qualities that rendered it deeply flawed and time-bound. In effect, Cruse had written an ideological tract, a political manifesto of sorts. Though informative, its importance did not and could not rest on its scholarly merits. After all, Cruse had interpreted the history of twentieth-century Afro-American intellectuals through the lens of a dogmatic ideology. In his quest to valorize a version of black nationalism as the correct ideology of the black intellectual, Cruse offered highly skewed interpretations of the intellectual and artistic projects of black thinkers. Non–black nationalist, black intellectuals, particularly anti–black nationalist, black intellectuals like those affiliated with the Communist Party, suffered the brunt of Cruse's tendentious analysis. *The Crisis of the Negro Intellectual* should be read as a polemical call to arms for black pundits. As a call to intellectual and artistic arms, the book was utterly captivating to a generation of engaged black intellectuals, though it remains unclear whether it actually influenced the beliefs and behavior of black intellectuals or provided them with an ideologically compelling legitimation for their existent political involvements.

The political and racial climates in the United States that greeted the publication of *The Crisis of the Negro Intellectual* only intensified the sense of political urgency within the black intellectual community. After years of optimism, the civil rights movement was by 1967 in decline for reasons having to do as much with its policy successes (such as the 1964 Civil Rights Act and the 1965 Voting Rights Act) as with the limitations of its policy outreach to incorporate and address the economic needs of impoverished blacks.

By 1967, the year of the book's publication, black "urban riots" had occurred in cities throughout the nation. Harlem exploded in 1964 and was followed one year later by a far larger and more lethal riot in the

Watts section of Los Angeles. These riots were singularly important as national public indicators of a rupture in the southern generated, church administered, civil rights vision of a peaceful black march to racial egalitarianism. As a result of the urban riots, the image of black political activists and, ultimately, black people was fundamentally altered within the national political discourse. The image of the black civil rights activist as a victim of "un-American" southern racist brutality was replaced by the image of the match-and-brick-wielding, anti-American, black militant violator of law and order. The former image had generated guilt in a significant portion of the white American populace. The latter image would generate white fear and resentment. The political and public policy responses emanating from these different moral depictions of blacks were quite different. The Johnson administration's interventions in behalf of black civil rights and economic impoverishment (the "war on poverty"), however flawed, were replaced by the "law and order," economically callous policies of Richard Nixon. Vice-President Hubert Humphrey's racial liberalism was replaced by Spiro T. Agnew's spiteful venom.

After the initial wave of the urban riots of the 1960s,[2] significant remnants of the black civil rights movement intelligentsia remained intact and attempted to recoup and develop new strategies for reaching out to nonsouthern black communities.[3] However, the deepening involvement of the United States in a war in Vietnam supplanted civil rights as the dominant liberal and state concern of the day. Surprisingly, the 1963 March on Washington would be the last major, organized, peaceful demonstration explicitly related to black civil rights that took place in the nation's capital during the 1960s. From the mid-1960s through the early 1970s, the major protest demonstrations in the District of Columbia would center around the involvement of the United States in the Vietnam War.

Black intellectuals oriented toward civil rights generally viewed the urban riots as indicators of mass despair in American cities. They argued that the civil rights era, and particularly the state response, had not gone far enough toward addressing the needs of those blacks who lived without the possibility of economic mobility in urban ghettos. In many respects, their explanations for those riots were reminiscent of Langston Hughes's poetic reflections on a dream deferred.[4] Moreover, the civil rights intelligentsia tended to see the riots as politically dysfunctional acts of desperation. Many within the circles of blacks oriented toward civil rights still believed that the United States had the potential to become a multiracial egalitarian society. Those within these ranks who did not actually believe that the United States was irretrievably headed toward becoming a multiracial democracy may at least have believed that such a social vision was the only morally viable one for Americans, white and black.

The black power/black nationalist wing of the black intelligentsia tended to view the black urban riots as political rebellions or even revolts.[5] To the extent that the anger and aggression of many of the rioters appeared to be directed against property and the protectors of property (that is, the police, the national guard, or the army), there were some who viewed these rebellions as protorevolutionary. According to this line of reasoning, black rioters were seen as rejecting the American Dream instead of as frustrated aspirants of the bourgeois life. The idea of rejecting American socioeconomic inclusion in behalf of a nebulously defined black separatist future gained a great deal of rhetorical currency within this sector of the black intelligentsia.

It is not clear to what degree these various black separatist ideologies incorporated a behavioral component. Some members of this black separatist wing of the intelligentsia did physically relocate to Africa.[6] However, one of the most prominent ways that the black nationalist/black separatist vision gained currency among the black intelligentsia was through the various attempts to develop separate black intellectual and artistic infrastructures. These efforts ranged from the attempt by LeRoi Jones to develop a black arts repertory school in Harlem to the creation of various black miniorganizations and caucuses, usually located within large, predominantly white academic organizations. For instance, black political scientists established such an organization, as did black sociologists and psychologists.[7] Nevertheless, the most important expansion of the black intellectual infrastructure that took place during this time was the creation of black studies programs and departments throughout American academia.[8]

In addition to this behavioral component, the black nationalist resurgence of the late 1960s and early 1970s went far beyond the mere establishment of intellectual infrastructures. The black nationalist mood was crucial at confronting the psychologically debilitating aspects of life for a subjugated black person in a racist society. It was, in effect, an attempt to generate among blacks and concerned whites a destigmatization of blackness. The attempt to valorize Africa was no small component of this effort.

While not proclaiming revolution, Cruse argues that black intellectuals needed to become more racially separatist in political and aesthetic orientations. He discounts political orientations that diverged from black nationalism as naive or self-defeating. Because of this narrow interpretation, Cruse can write as if most black intellectuals have been detrimental or irrelevant to the political struggles of twentieth-century black Americans. For Cruse, the political cul-de-sac of black intellectuals stemmed from their misreading of American history. He argues that black intellectuals were pursuing a vision of an integrated America when in fact American cultural norms were deeply embedded in ethnic pluralism.[9]

Black intellectuals have a long history of participating in Afro-American activist politics. W. E. B. Du Bois, one of the founders of the National Association for the Advancement of Colored People (NAACP), remains a model of highbrow political engagement.[10] Ida Wells-Barnett[11] and Monroe Trotter,[12] intellectuals in the guise of militant journalists, had engaged in the quest to raise the political consciousness of dormant and dominated black populations. Legal theorist Charles Houston used his Harvard Law School education and the deanship at Howard University School of Law to train a cadre of black lawyers in those techniques and strategies that would one day confront and overturn *Plessy v. Ferguson*.[13] Mamie and Kenneth Clark, two pioneer black psychologists, committed their research skills to help strengthen the case of the NAACP in pursuit of the *Brown v. Board of Education* ruling.[14] Pauli Murray, poet, lawyer, and pioneer female Episcopal priest, helped to generate a black presence within the early moments of the feminist movement that arose during the 1960s.[15]

On the other hand, "nonactivist" black intellectuals have played a crucial part in Afro-American politics in the guise of thinkers, ideologues, and conveyers of knowledge. Historian Carter G. Woodson's impact on black social and political life was immense via the very fact that he spent his life rescuing the complexity of black history and cultural identity from the simplifications of the dominant American racist depictions of blacks, blackness, and Africa.[16] In some ways the example of Carter G. Woodson raises questions about the appropriateness of an engaged versus a disengaged dichotomy for Afro-American intellectual life. Reclusive and secluded scholars who were engaged in serious antiracist research were inadvertently engaged.

Even the more technical sector of the black intelligentsia has not been at a loss concerning how to place itself in the service of the needs of the broader black community. When one thinks of those black intellectuals who did not participate in public sphere politics but who, for instance, were competent teachers at various black colleges or segregated high schools, one realizes that many black intellectuals, broadly defined, were quite well integrated in the struggles and social uplift mission of the broader black community. In many respects, Cruse's "crisis" was a sectarian ploy. He wanted to frame the issues of black intellectual life and politics along a rather simpleminded axis between black nationalism and integrationism. Needless to say, he endorsed the former as the only authentic emancipatory outlook for creative black intellectuals. Instead of an analysis of an ongoing crisis in black intellectual life, Cruse was actually laying the intellectual groundwork for the emergence of a dominant black nationalist wing of intellectuals.

Ironically, the events of the late 1960s that set the stage for the emergence of *The Crisis of the Negro Intellectual* as a linchpin of black intellectual activity also became the first implicit test case for the Cruse thesis. With the benefit of a twenty-five-year hindsight it is clear that the Cruse thesis did not, in fact, work. This black nationalist moment quickly became mired in black parochialism; cathartic/therapeutic, ethnic cheerleading; and sectarianism. It produced little of lasting intellectual and artistic value relative to its overblown, insipid claims. Furthermore, black nationalist intellectual opportunism ran amok. Perhaps this was indicative of a degree of naivete in Cruse's formulations of the crisis of black intellectuals. Simply put, Cruse had underestimated the degree to which the most vehement black nationalist intellectual was fundamentally American. As such, these intellectuals were often as committed to material acquisition and status attainment as anyone within the academy. That is, many of the black intellectuals who embraced black nationalism had little authentic commitment to black nationalism as an oppositional form of politics. Instead they appropriated nationalism because they thought that it was a rhetoric and ideology that could generate substantive benefits from the academy and/or the state. The willingness of many black intellectuals to join the black nationalist bandwagon often stemmed from their desires to legitimate themselves to the broader black activist community and to subsequently gain access to the mobility that the political system offered to black nationalist intellectuals in response to the maintenance of black quietude in urban areas. Despite its militant-sounding rhetoric, black nationalism became an ideology of economic and status mobility for bourgeois intellectuals. Martin Kilson perceived the self-interested nature of the black nationalist identity for many black intellectuals. He wrote:

> Some professionals are adopting a Black Power ideological format not with the intent of preparing themselves for service to self-governing urban black communities but to make themselves more visible to the white establishment, which is not at all adverse to offering such persons good jobs as alternatives to Black Power. The more viable Negro businessmen are also simulating the Black Power advocates who have virtually no control over this use of their political style by the professional and business black bourgeoisie, which means the Black Power advocates will eventually lose the payoff potential of nationalist politics. If so . . . the Negro lower classes, whose riots legitimize Black Power, will be joined by the Black Power advocates in holding the bag—with nothing in it save a lot of therapeutic miscellany.[17]

Once black nationalism ceased to be able to generate legitimacy for bourgeois intellectuals and failed to fuel job mobility, it began to recede within black intellectual ranks. Whether for pragmatic or opportunistic reasons, black intellectuals altered their ideologies. Cruse had taken insufficient account of the social class location of traditional black intellectuals and their resultant material aspirations. He took their nationalist rhetoric at face value as if black intellectuals were simply disaffiliated vessels carrying around enslaving or emancipatory ideas. How else, for instance, could he have assumed that the espousing of black nationalism by traditional black intellectuals actually meant that they were fundamentally concerned about the broader black community? In effect,

Cruse failed to incorporate a sociology of knowledge formulation into his discussion. For instance, even if Cruse wanted to place the blame for black integrationist-minded intellectuals on their supposed Jewish intellectual bosses, he does so without any sociological analysis. What did these so-called flunky black intellectuals and artists supposedly receive as payoffs for opposing black nationalism? This is a question that Cruse must but does not answer. Instead Cruse's analysis of nationalism gets mired in his own naive nationalistic framework. Like all nationalism, black nationalism is predicated upon a reified consciousness. In this instance, all blacks are thought to share intrinsically a collective interest as a result of their blackness. Moreover, Cruse added to this belief the assumption that blacks shared a common culture and cultural heritage that needed to be intellectually mined by black philosophers and artists.

The black nationalist movement of the late 1960s and early 1970s ultimately succeeded in establishing black nationalism as a hegemonic ideology within the Afro-American intelligentsia, at least for a moment. Black intellectuals who were not nationalist were consistently scrutinized and even labeled ethnically traitorous. Writing in 1969, Amiri Baraka, a doyen of the black nationalist moment in Afro-American arts and letters, proclaimed: "The Negro artist who is not a nationalist at this late date is a white artist, even without knowing it. He is creating death snacks, for and out of dead stuff. What he does will not matter because it is in the shadow, connected with the shadow and will die when the shadow dies."[18] Unfortunately, the Cruse text and the equally simplistic aesthetic formulations of Baraka and other black ideologues became central to discussions of Afro-American intellectual life. Usually such discussions centered around the feasibility of a black aesthetic.[19] In the process, traditions of sophisticated debates about the linkages pro and con between artistic creativity and political engagement were scuttled in behalf of one-dimensional diatribes about the "correct" ideology for black intellectuals. Lost in these pedestrian discussions was a central question for black intellectuals and artists: How is it possible for black American intellectuals and artists to sustain artistically viable creative angsts and disciplines in the face of the sometimes overwhelming debilitations and influences of racial subjugation? To what extent does the political situation shape the ability of the Afro-American intellectual to realize his or her creativity? Whereas Cruse claims that the goal of the black artist is to produce ideologically correct depictions of black life, a more substantive goal is to produce artistically sophisticated depictions of black life.

For over forty years Ralph Ellison has stood as an artistic beacon warning against simplistic understandings of the creative process, Afro-American or otherwise. Long before Harold Bloom put pen to paper, it was the Malraux-influenced Ellison who taught us that artist/intellectuals were only as good as the artistic ancestors they claimed and used as measuring rods and inspirations. Furthermore, he told us that the exclusive way to ultimately critique and transcend a weak text was not through ideologically condemning it but through writing a better book.

Readers might describe the following reflections on Ralph Ellison as Janus-faced. They would not be wrong to do so. Throughout this commentary on Ellison, I am engaged in silent argument with two thematic tendencies employed in many studies of black intellectuals. I refer to these antagonistic tendencies as (1) the hyperpoliticized and (2) the depoliticized. Not only do these thematic centers represent two major tendencies in Afro-American cultural studies, but their binary antagonism to each other has mistakenly led critics to believe that in using the typology they have comprehensively exhausted the terrain.

In confronting hyperpoliticized discussions of black intellectuals, I am quietly arguing with those like Harold Cruse who tend to think that all Afro-American artistic and intellectual activity is reducible to political intentions. Cruse represents a black nationalist variant of the hyperpoliticized. This black intellectual sector had its most recent heyday during the black nationalist moment of the late 1960s and early 1970s. Yet the hyperpoliticized student of Afro-American intellectuals need not be a black nationalist. After all, Amiri Baraka's current advocacy of a dogmatic Marxist-Leninism generates hyperpoliticized readings of black artists today in much the same manner that his antiwhite, black nationalism of the 1960s once did.[20] In both instances simplicity reigns.

In addition, I am attempting to engage those students of Afro-American intellectual life who either have taken politics out of their interpretations of black intellectual activity or have reduced the field of artistic political activity to textual practices. Proclaiming a willingness to engage complexity, these students of Afro-American cultural studies seem all too willing, for instance, to attribute a text of such a consciously political writer as Richard Wright to the author's wish to comment silently on Zora Neale Hurston. Wright's explicit desire to speak to the social situation in which he lived is granted secondary importance to the ways in which Wright supposedly responded to and kept an Afro-American artistic tradition alive.

In this short study I intend to utilize the example of Ralph Ellison as an intellectual case study in order to highlight some of the political and aesthetic dilemmas that ambitious, traditional Afro-American intellectuals have confronted during the twentieth century. I am interested in both the strategies that Ellison employed in order to learn to become an excellent writer and the ways that these strategies intersected with certain political choices he made. In the process, I hope to bring politics back into the discussion of Ellison and to do so without subjecting him to dogmatic ideological formulations.

I explicitly do not claim that my study of Ellison is exhaustive. Most significantly, I do not engage in a literary analysis of *Invisible Man*. This omission is not an oversight. As a student of the sociology of black intellectual life, I am less concerned with the substantive meanings of the artistic and intellectual productions of particular black artists than with the ideological contexts that helped to shape their intellectual outlooks. Conversely I am quite concerned about those material forces that an individual black intellectual had to face in order to engage in his or her creative activity.

Though not exhaustive, this study is novel. In order to obtain a more substantive understanding of Ellison's politics, I have elevated his explicit social and political writings to a status they do not normally occupy in discussions of his ouvre. In confronting Ellison's politics, I inevitably cross over into a discussion of his public life and personal political engagements. In bringing his life into view, I am of course treading on murky grounds. This is not a biography, literary or otherwise. I have neither interviewed Ellison nor his close associates. However, when I did discover something about Ellison's life that appears to shed light on his intellectual development and political choices, I could not but help mention it. What, for instance, would we do if we discovered that a male defender of feminism was a wife beater at home? Do we ignore the latter in behalf of proclaiming his published work the sole event worthy of study? Or do we let his behavior actually inform our understanding of his political commitments and practices? In either case, such discussions ultimately expose the actual sloppiness of people's lives. This text is a plea to reinvigorate our abilities to deal with sloppiness. Ironically, the enticements of the hyperpoliticized and the depoliticized analytical strategies may lie in the fact that they render unnecessary such confrontations with life's loose ends.

Throughout the 1960s and 1970s, Ellison remained true to his values and political beliefs. He refused to change opportunistically or to appear to have changed with the times in behalf of closing ranks with the new black arts movement. A committed integrationist, Ellison continued to champion a view of America as a paradoxical, new world, mulatto society. Black Americans were not Africans on the North American continent, nor for that matter were white Americans simply transplanted Europeans. Instead, black Americans were culturally part white, and white Americans were culturally part black. The history and politics of the United States had created a new, culturally heterogeneous people.

The Ellisonian concept of American culture, though easy to trace historically and to document empirically, was undoubtedly at times difficult to defend politically in a nation in which racial politics has seldom been as complex or fluid as its cultural identity. After all, the cultural hybrid nature of white Americans had not succeeded in inspiring them to rid America of racism and racial subjugation. To claim interracial cultural cross-fertilization within a society in which socially, politically, and economically based racial differences were so distinct may have appeared somewhat disingenuous.

Ellison was a deviant in another sense, however. He refused to let the highly politicized moments of the civil rights movement and black power era determine his intellectual/artistic style. That is, Ellison had long believed that he artistically created best when he was least actively engaged in politics. He refused to accept the popular claim that the only viable and ethnically legitimate black intellectual style is a politically engaged one. Within black intellectual circles, this aspect of Ellison was perhaps more difficult for him to defend than his refusal to adopt black nationalism.

By the mid-1970s the hegemonic status of black nationalism within the black intelligentsia began to decline. Black intellectuals once again began to wrestle with many of the issues raised years earlier by Ellison.

This time, however, the neo-Ellisonian revalorization of black cultural heterogeneity was merged with a Cruse-influenced belief in the necessity of political engagement. In addition, the cultures of the African diaspora were subsequently included in the idea of Afro-American cultural heterogeneity.

THEORIZING THE BLACK INTELLECTUAL CONUNDRUM

Amidst this flowing in Afro-American literary studies and intellectual history, however, the sociological study of the black intellectuals has lagged drastically. It is my intention to begin to address this lacuna in Afro-American cultural studies. Through a sociological approach to the study of black intellectuals, I am able to situate them materially in various political formations and social contexts.

The tradition of sociological studies of intellectuals is a rich one within Euro-American sociology. Names of seminal scholars in this area include Karl Mannheim, Alvin Gouldner, Pierre Bourdieu, Edward Shils, Robert Merton, Lewis Coser, Daniel Bell, Norman Birnbaum, Seymour Martin Lipset, Zygmunt Bauman, Robert Nisbet, and Raymond Aron, among others.[21] This approach tends to treat intellectuals as a semi-self-conscious social strata, a knowledge elite. Because of the language, analytical, and information-processing skills that intellectuals possess, they play certain key roles in the social order. In studying the sociology of the intelligentsia, we seek to understand the various roles that intellectuals traditionally play (that is, as legitimators of power or as critics of power) and to link these roles to the various occupations that intellectuals tend to inhabit (journalists, teachers, and propagandists). The quality of the diversity of the roles intellectuals are allowed to assume has ultimately something to do with their political behavior as a group.

A fundamental assumption of this study is that traditional Afro-American intellectuals, like all traditional intellectuals, have as one of their priorities, if not their highest priority, the reproduction of themselves as intellectuals. Black writers want to write; black painters want to paint. Whatever fuels the time and space to write or paint becomes a priority for intellectuals. One of the fundamental tensions of twentieth-century traditional Afro-American intellectual life is precisely that the black intellectuals' quests to reproduce themselves as intellectuals were severely hindered by the viciousness of white American racism. During this same period, black American intellectuals did not have ready access to grants, fellowships, research positions at elite universities, or even memberships on the editorial boards of prominent American intellectual journals. Simultaneously, these black intellectuals also had to confront the inability of their ethnic group to sustain ambitious, traditional artistic and intellectual activity. For most of the twentieth century the broader black community neither had the resources nor the desire to give a high priority to the funding of traditional intellectual and artistic activities. As such, blacks for the most part did not create a sufficiently large and diverse intellectual infrastructure of journals, theaters, record production companies, and other cultural endeavors to fill the void left by racist white intellectual exclusions. This is quite understandable given the dire plight of many if not most blacks throughout the first half of the twentieth century. However, as a result, black intellectuals and artists were caught in a frozen status and an economic limbo. Moreover, black audiences were often incapable of functioning critically for black artistic and intellectual works. Reflect on the case of a black opera singer who during the 1930s was denied access to the Metropolitan Opera and other major opera companies in the United States. The black community could not provide her with a qualitatively similar alternative opera network. The low economic and educational attainment of most blacks during the 1930s restricted their exposure to this and numerous other non-Afro-American folk art forms. Consequently, black Americans could provide neither a critical listening audience nor the necessary financial backing to support such highly trained singers.

The condition of being simultaneously denied access to the mainstream (read white-controlled) intellectual resources and critical audiences while being a member of an ethnic group that did not have the resources and/or educational attainment sufficient to sustain serious traditional intellectual activity placed traditional black intellectuals in a unique vice. I refer to this precarious betwixt-between social status as *social marginality*.[22] For most of the twentieth century, black traditional intellectuals have been socially marginal to the white and black communities.

In hopes of navigating this problematic social situation black intellectuals developed concerted strategies for creating functional intellectual/artistic creative spaces. Strategies that are employed by black intellectuals in order to navigate black artistic social marginality will be called *social marginality facilitators*. Regardless of form, the social marginality facilitator has ultimately one purpose: to increase, protect, and nurture the individual's artistic and intellectual "space." For instance, Richard Wright used his membership in the Communist Party U.S.A. as a social marginality facilitator. While Wright was attracted to Marxism, he was more attracted to the idea of becoming a writer. Where else but the John Reed clubs of the Communist Party could a black, southern, high school dropout have his writing examined and taken seriously by published writers? In effect, the Communist Party provided Wright with the material necessities of a young intellectual life. Ellison, early in his writing career, also used the Communist Party as a social marginality facilitator. However, he did not do so to the extent that Wright did, for Ellison had already spent three years in college. That is, he was less dependent on the Communists for an intellectual apprenticeship.

Social marginality facilitators can come in many guises. Expatriation has been a major social marginality facilitator for some twentieth-century black intellectuals. Black writers have become expatriates in order to obtain access to an environment that affirms their racial and artistic identities. Other black artists, such as Shakespearean actors and opera singers, became expatriates because they were simply not allowed to practice their craft in the United States.[23] Living the bohemian life was another frequently used social marginality facilitator for black intellectuals. Black intellectuals in need of a supportive, stimulating, and nurturing environment often journeyed to bohemia, a place culturally quite distant from the black and white mainstream societies. Jean Toomer, Claude McKay, Bob Kaufman, and LeRoi Jones, among others, utilized this social marginality facilitator.

The problems confronting the black intellectual in twentieth-century America are not solely material. One of the most debilitating vices imprisoning black intellectuals centers around the way in which America has morally navigated the race question. Among the most crippling and pervasive ideological constructs that blacks have had to face is the idea of the victim status.[24]

The victim status is a metaphorical paradigm that describes an ideological discourse that mediates the conflict for mutual recognition that lies at the heart of the oppressed-oppressor interrelationship. As an ideological discourse, the victim status establishes moral guidelines for this relationship. The victim status hinges on the desire of the victimized to obtain from the victimizer recognition of their victimized status and the willingness of the victimizer both to accept the victimized as their creation and to grant to the victimized the desired recognition. In the process, the humanity of the victimized is supposedly affirmed, but the superiority of the victimizer is not challenged. Moreover, the humanity and goodness of the victimizer is affirmed, for the victimized could not rationally appeal to an amoral or immoral victimizer. In helping the victim, the victimizer appears to act in a moral manner precisely because his or her actions are not perceived as self-interested. Concerning this, Orlando Patterson wrote, "Why should the man who has enslaved and exploited you respond to your cry unless, far from being an immoral tyrant, he has more than a spark of magnanimity? Indeed, the greater the appeal or demand for redress from the oppressor, the greater the implied concession of the moral superiority of the oppressor. For the latter has nothing to gain and everything to lose by releasing his constraints on the ability of those he has oppressed to compete with him equally."[25] For the victim status to emerge, the victimizer must experience guilt and/or shame (but sometimes fear) over his or her treatment of the victimized. Though the victim status demands of the victimizer more than simple acknowledgment of responsibility for the plight of the victimized, it does not demand of the victimizer a desire to relinquish control over the victimized. The victim status is an inherently unequal relationship, one premised on the fact that the victimized is necessary for the existence of the victimizer. The victimizer is able to enjoy the life he or she lives in part because of his or her exploitation of the victimized. As a result, the best moral posture that one can expect for a victimizer locked into a victim status relationship with the victimized is paternalism. Through paternalism, the victimized can often receive material benefits and economic improvement. Paternalism cannot grant the subjugated emancipation.

The victim status is a metaphor for an ideological discourse that mediates the political, economic, and psychological relationships between oppressed and oppressor. It is not an empirical description of the machinations of an exploitative material relationship. The presence of the victim status in no way informs us of the quality of the existent oppression. In a late capitalist society like the United States, the victim status is but one major component of the hegemonic discourses that legitimate racial inequality (as well as class and gender inequalities) and ultimately shape and stymie the forms of oppositional discourses. More precisely, the victim status may be a primary hegemonic discourse for morally generating voluntary acceptance of inequality by oppressed groups. Such groups are encouraged to enter a victim status relationship through material inducements. Such material benefits, which might improve the living conditions of the oppressed, are offered in lieu of authentic political equality or self-determination. Because the victim status is an ideological discourse, we can readily perceive that all subjugated people in the United States do not necessarily occupy a victim status. As stated earlier, the victim status can only arise when the victimized seek recognition of their victimization from the victimizer and the victimizer grants such recognition. But not all who are victimized seek such recognition, nor are all who seek recognition granted it.

The victim status sacrifices moral autonomy for social acceptance and material gain. In appealing to the justice and morality of the oppressor, the oppressed often participate in the legitimation of their own oppression. Guilt might result in increases in benefits given to blacks, but it cannot generate equality. By its very definition it presupposes dependency.

The dialectical relationship between victim and victimizer has been explored in the writings of Frantz Fanon, Albert Memmi, Jean-Paul Sartre, and Paulo Freire, among others.[26] Revising the seminal arguments of Hegel and Nietzsche, these individuals have developed an ideal type of the victim as one locked in a struggle with the victimizer for recognition. In this struggle, the victims often desire to be like the victimizer. More precisely, the victimizer is seen in the eyes of the victims as being the "free person." As such, freedom becomes associated with the dominance of other human beings.

The victims are actually torn between hatred and envy of the victimizer. In desiring to be like the victimizer, the victims internalize values that are antithetical to their freedom, for in effect, they valorize the victimizer for denying their own freedom. In this sense, the victims are torn between their hatred and envy of the victimizer. The state of being torn is one in which the victims simultaneously adhere to their own values (the desire to be free and the values that support that desire) and the victimizer's values (the desire to deny freedom and the values that rationalize this domination). I call this state of being torn the *victim status syndrome* and consider it a primary component of twentieth-century Afro-American ethnic identity.

When trapped within the victim status, black intellectuals become incapable of realizing their authentic creativity. Too concerned about white recognition, they shy away from self-affirmation of their creative products unless these have already been certified or praised by the "proper" or authoritative white gatekeepers. The early protest fiction of Richard Wright was locked in a victim status syndrome precisely because it was intended as a mechanism to induce white guilt. Because Wright was intent on generating white guilt and, later, white fear, he sacrificed a complex discussion of black life.[27] Black victim status intellectuals often use criteria for validating the existence of their people that are not only derived from the victimizer but serve to rationalize further their own inferior status. For example, the widely practiced attempt to predicate black American pride on a knowledge of the great kings and kingdoms in African history is a victim status appeal. This argument assumes that the greatness of a people lies in their ability to conquer and rule others, which after all simply validates the greatness of a Western world that dominated the black world. Instead of proudly proclaiming that we too have tyrants, black intellectuals might want to help delegitimize empires as the basis of human pride. To do so, however, would necessitate stepping outside the oppressor's values, an act of freedom that might sever the victim from the victimizer's umbilical cord.

One of the enticements of the victim status for some black intellectuals is that those groups that occupy a victim status are granted increased moral authority. In a culture influenced by Jewish and Christian values, the victim is considered morally superior. The victim possesses a valued cultural status. It is not surprising that groups fight over access to the victim status via "who-has-suffered-more" contests. James Baldwin was a quintessential black victim-status intellectual.[28] A moralist, Baldwin claimed to have superior moral vision on the basis of his suffering.

The intellectual problem with the victim status is that it is a parasitic status. For blacks, it is utterly dependent on recognition from whites. All of one's energy is invested in obtaining this recognition as opposed to perfecting one's craft or pursuing one's ideas regardless of where they lead.

The black intellectual who tries to step outside the logic of the victim status syndrome in whatever form it has assumed in his or her genre and historical moment will be called *ethnically marginal*.[29] Such individuals are in pursuit of greater artistic freedom and human agency than that which is typically allowed under the hegemonic victim-status ideology. I use the term *ethnically marginal* to highlight their deviancy within their ethnic group. As is the case with social marginality, there are *ethnic marginality facilitators*. An ethnic marginality facilitator is an ideology or way of thinking that provides the black intellectual with access to a creative space free or freer of the dictates of a prevailing victim status. Jean Toomer, for instance, used the ideas of the Russian mystic-philosopher Gurdjieff to facilitate access to an artistic/intellectual space in which the society's prevailing racial definitions took on secondary importance. As such he was able, at least in his own mind, to relocate himself outside the prevailing ideological confines of Afro-American art dominant during his creative life.[30] Many black intellectuals have used Marxism to facilitate a redefinition of their identity vis-à-vis an Afro-American victim status. Marxism undermined claims for the special victim status of blacks and instead made the black situation part of a broader class assault on the capitalist domination. Marxism allowed one to struggle in behalf of the emancipation of black Americans without getting mired in pleas to the "master" for recognition. It fundamentally redefined the relationship between the oppressed and the oppressor in such a way that the dependency of the oppressed was no longer an issue. It is important to note that an adherence to Marxism as an ethnic marginality facilitator sometimes overlapped with an adherence to the Communist Party as a social marginality facilitator. Yet, this need not be the case, for there were some black intellectuals who were attracted to Marxism but who did not want to divorce themselves from the black community to the extent that membership in the Communist Party signified. One such figure was the sociologist Oliver Cox.[31] The case of Ellison is instructive, for Ellison has long recognized the dual problems of social marginality and the victim status. Moreover, he has developed unique responses to each. Yet his responses are also politically problematic.

Through the study of Ellison, we can raise questions about the "responsibilities" of black intellectuals who are not overtly engaged in political affairs. To engage Ellison is to implicitly critique Cruse. Is authentic black intellectual and artistic life necessarily circumscribed by politics? In many respects, Ellison represents a fundamentally important phenomenon in black intellectual life—the intellectual who believes that disengagement from politics best serves his creative ambitions. Political disengagement may appear to some as a luxury that intellectual members of subjugated groups can ill afford. According to this argument, the creative ambitions of the individual intellectual become secondary to the political needs of his or her subjugated group. The appeal of this logic is somewhat self-evident, for it is able to define black artistic ambitions as inherently privativistic unless they are placed in the service of a greater goal. But what if one believes à la Ellison that one's private artistic creations inherently advance the status of the entire group, not to mention the nation at large or even humanity?

Certainly black Americans stand to benefit from the active political engagement of their intellectual strata. What this involvement would actually mean in terms of changed life chances for black Americans we do not and cannot know. However, there is little reason to assume that a fiction writer and essayist like Ellison would have held any of the keys to black advancement had he chosen to become more involved in activist black politics.

Ellison has argued that ambitious Afro-American intellectuals must submit to the same grueling journey, radical self-doubt, and creative anxiety that all fine Western artists have embarked on for centuries. Furthermore, due to racism and/or white paternalism, black intellectuals and artists will often be treated as if they need not undergo the same confrontation with the creative abyss as their white peers. Such claims are often predicated on the assumption that the black American is effortlessly creative. Black artists, Ellison reminds us, not only have to engage simultaneously in those practices and disciplines that allow them to perfect their craft, but given their social and political marginality in the United States, black intellectuals must be exceptionally self-motivated and resilient. The serious black artist must be nothing less than heroic, a committed human being forged out an act of will. It is my contention that the Ellisonian strategy for confronting social marginality and the victim status has been nothing less than a call for heroic individualism. In *The Hero and The Blues*, Albert Murray formulated a useful definition of heroism.

Heroism, which like the sword is nothing if not steadfast, is measured in terms of the stress and strain it can endure and the magnitude and complexity of the obstacles it overcomes. Thus difficulties and vicissitudes which beset the potential hero on all sides not only threaten his existence and jeopardize his prospects; they also, by bringing out the best in him, serve his purpose. They make it possible for him to make something of himself. Such is the nature of every confrontation in the context of heroic action.[32]

Black intellectual life is ripe with heroic possibilities. To the extent that there are racist obstacles placed in the way of the black individual's intellectual and artistic development, racial oppression functions as an inspiring landscape for transcendence. As Ellison and Murray might remark, the black intellectual is locked in a dynamic state of antagonistic cooperation with the forces that would deny him a chance to develop his craft. To the extent that fine artistic transcendence is inherently an individual's initiative, Ellison believed that the ambitious black artist must be a heroic individualist. It is therefore not surprising that one of Ellison's intellectual heroes was André Malraux. Malraux was a larger-than-life figure who not only wrote about heroic transcendence but actually tried to compose a heroic life.

It is significant that I am choosing today to write about Ellison, for the example of Ellison demands intense scrutiny, time, and a reflective space. Of all major contemporary black intellectual figures, Ellison probably comes least to mind when we think of politically engaged intellectuals. Yet Ellison's example raises questions about the artistic costs and viability of political involvement that should at least be considered by thoughtful black intellectuals and artists. Because of the lull in mass black political involvement, the black intellectual community has the momentary breathing space to reflect on and reconsider its roles and activities during the political movements of the 1960s and 1970s. Perhaps in so doing, those interested in contemporary and future political engagement might better serve their communities and themselves.

On the other hand, those who were swept up in the euphoria of political engagement and relinquished their creative abilities as artists might well reconsider their future postures vis-à-vis mass political involvement. The issue is not that black intellectuals are less needed today by the black community and America than they were twenty-five years ago. They are needed, sorely needed. However, politically conscious black intellectuals need to engage in consistent reflection about their duties, allegiances, and ambitions. As long as the black community remains oppressed, traditional black intellectuals and artists may have their ethnic legitimacy brought into question. Such assaults can be generated within or outside the black community. Sometimes they can be quite debilitating. Moreover, black artists and intellectuals may confront various levels of self-generated doubt about the utility of their enterprises vis-à-vis black America or the world at large. I cannot provide any systematic insights into how to address what are ultimately very personal confrontations of fundamental importance. Yet, these reflections on Ellison are part of a larger project intent upon analyzing the ways that some prominent intellectuals have dealt with some of the enduring hurdles facing Afro-American thinkers and artists. Ellison, an extraordinarily reflective artist, offers as good a place as any to begin this journey.

The name Ralph Ellison reverberates throughout contemporary Afro-American intellectual discourse. Hated or revered, Ellison is considered a formidable foe or ally. Of living Afro-American writers Ellison's influence among his black contemporaries is unsurpassed except perhaps by Amiri Baraka and, now, Toni Morrison. He has long been a standard-bearer for black fiction writers, an imprimatur of ethnic excellence. The significance of Ellison is quite remarkable insofar as he has not been particularly prolific. Though best known as a novelist, Ellison has published only one novel in over fifty years of writing.

Ellison's status within black arts and letters was established in 1952 with the publication of *Invisible Man*. *Invisible Man* was not immediately celebrated in all circles. As Jacqueline Covo has noted in *The Blinking Eye: Ralph Waldo Ellison and His American, French, German, and Italian Critics, 1952–1971*, most early reviews of the novel raised questions about its technical competence.[1] Some reviewers claimed that it was poorly written. Few engaged its thesis. The brilliance of the "invisibility" theme, when coupled with Ellison's master craftsmanship, ultimately propelled the novel to a celebrated status within most major American literary circles. Gradually Ellison rose from an unknown, poverty-stricken writer to a prominent national intellectual figure. *Invisible Man* was awarded the 1953 National Book Award. Ellison, the first Afro-American to receive this prestigious literary award, had indeed "arrived." Though Richard Wright, the dean of Afro-American literature and the most celebrated black novelist of the period, was alive and writing in France, Ellison became for many the new standard of excellence for black American writing. Given the racial parochialism of the broader intellectual community, Ellison was at times relegated to a corner inhabited only by Negro writers, leading *Time* magazine to "honor" him by calling him the "best of all U.S. Negro writers."[2] In discussing *Invisible Man*, Nathan Scott has written, "It was of course, in the spring of that year that Ralph Ellison's novel *Invisible Man* burst upon the scene, and the astonishing authority of its art and of the systematic vision of the world which this art expressed immediately won for the book a preeminence which in the intervening years, far from being in any way diminished, has so consolidated itself that it is today universally regarded as an established classic of modern American literature."[3] Ellison's admirers often mention the 1965 *Book Week* poll of two hundred writers, critics, and editors that named *Invisible Man* as "the most distinguished work published in the last twenty years."[4] Even Norman Mailer, whose "quick and expensive comments" were sharply condemnatory of "most talents in the room," wrote admiringly of Ellison,

> That Ralph Ellison is very good is dull to say. He is essentially a hateful writer; when the line of his satire is pure, he writes so perfectly

that one can never forget the experience of reading him—it is like holding a live electric wire in one's hand.

. . . Where Ellison can go, I have no idea. His talent is too exceptional to allow for casual predictions, and if one says that the way for Ellison may be to adventure out into the difficult and conceivably more awful invisibility of the white man—well, it is a mistake to write prescriptions for a novelist as gifted as Ellison.[5]

A decade after the publication of *Invisible Man*, Ellison published a collection of essays, *Shadow and Act*, which revealed a brilliant critical intellect.[6] The book contained previously published essays and interviews and a few new essays. The subject matter ranged from jazz musicians and gospel/blues singers to a review of Gunnar Myrdal's *An American Dilemma*. It contained essays about the culture of the Negro and a condensed version of Ellison's contribution to the now famous exchange with Irving Howe. Ellison was not only a fine fiction writer but also a precise interpreter of American literary culture and the writer's craft. *Shadow and Act* contains the most comprehensive statements yet collected of Ellison's views of Afro-American life and folk culture and their relationship to the Afro-American writer. Within some intellectual/artistic circles, this collection of essays has obtained the status of a classic, and rightly so.[7] Stanley Edgar Hyman celebrated it from his central vantage point within the white literary establishment. In his review "Ralph Ellison in Our Time," Hyman wrote, "*Shadow and Act* is a monument of integrity, a banner proclaiming 'the need to keep literary standards high'. In his insight into the complexity of American experience, Ralph Ellison is the profoundest cultural critic that we have, and his hard doctrine of freedom, responsibility, and fraternity is a wisdom rare in our time."[8]

In 1986 Ellison published his second collection of nonfiction essays, *Going to the Territory*.[9] Like *Shadow and Act*, this collection consisted primarily of previously published material. Enduring Ellisonian themes such as the complexity of Afro-American identity, the ironies of American racial mores, and the humanizing disciplines of the arts mark this collection as an extension of *Shadow and Act*. Because *Going to the Territory* was recognizably and predictably Ellisonian in a way that the first essay collection could not have been, it did not generate the immediate and intense awe of *Shadow and Act*. Ellison's reading audience had come to expect nothing less than profound and elegant writing. *Going to the Territory* would not disappoint them. Yet the essay collection was issued to a public punch-drunk over rumors and false announcements of the forthcoming publication of the second novel. The reception for *Going to the Territory* was almost anticlimactic. Still, David Bradley in his review of the collection wrote, "The essays never fail to be elegantly written, beautifully composed and intellectually sophisticated. The personality that emerges from the pages is witty, literate, endearingly modest, delightfully puckish. So much so that, while one cannot completely forgive Ellison for not writing that novel we've all been waiting for, one does start to wonder if we have not been waiting for the wrong thing."[10]

Ellison's staying power in Afro-American intellectual discourse has almost as much to do with his nonfictional writing on Afro-American life, culture, and politics as with *Invisible Man*. While *Invisible Man* is often recognized as an unsurpassed accomplishment in Afro-American letters, Ellison's views concerning the identity of black Americans and his thoughts on the role of the black writer have generated heated controversies, particularly within Afro-American cultural studies.

Writing about Ellison can be an intimidating exercise. Making claims about him is difficult for fear of imprecision, and worse, prolonged rebuttals, if not from Ellison then from one of his legion of admirers. Ellison is a master of ambivalence and nuance. Not only does this make it difficult for critics to reconstruct and criticize his arguments, but it also allows Ellison to write extensively about the most commonplace occurrences in his life and endow them with extreme significance and mythic proportions. Such embellishments, he claims, are the writer's prerogative:

> For we select neither our parents, our race nor our nation; these occur to us out of the love, the hate, the circumstances, the fate, of others. But we do become writers out of an act of will, out of an act of choice; a dim, confused and ofttimes regrettable choice, perhaps, but choice nevertheless. And what happens thereafter causes all those experiences which occurred before we began to function as writers to take on a special quality of uniqueness. If this does not happen then as far as writing goes, the experiences have been misused. If we do not

make of them a value, if we do not transform them into forms and images of meaning which they did not possess before, then we have failed as artists.[11]

At present one cannot challenge Ellison's interpretations of his life, and no one may be able to do so as long as he is alive. A biography of Ellison remains to be written.[12] Much of the significance that Ellison attributes to various experiences from his life appears both contrived and an after-the-fact assertion that sounds plausible to us precisely because we presuppose sensitivity and irony in the life of the author of a novel as impressive as *Invisible Man*. Are we really to believe that Ellison learned how to hunt birds from reading Hemingway?[13] Perhaps, but is this not a significant tale only because it allows Ellison to romanticize the intensity of his commitment to literature—that he would literally live by the novel? That Ellison weaves fictions around his identity and the identities of other Afro-Americans is significant for our analysis insofar as the mythmaking dynamic at work throughout his nonfiction writings appropriates specific forms and embodies a peculiar sociopolitical vision.[14]

Ellison's ability to impart intrigue and complexity into the most commonplace occurrences in his life is rendered even more powerful by the fact that his tales simultaneously appeal to and negate the hidden but deep-seated stereotypical racist imagery of the Negro lurking in the back of the reader's imagination. The images he confronts have long rendered black people one-dimensional, dominated by racial concerns, and most importantly, void of irony.[15] Not only is *Invisible Man* a protest against the fiction genre of Richard Wright and his simplification of black life, but Ellison's description of his own life is a protest against the depiction of Wright's life in *Black Boy*.

Ellison spends an enormous amount of energy controlling his public image and has been very successful at doing so. An extraordinary perfectionist, Ellison refuses to grant spontaneous interviews unless he can revise the final transcript. Yet these interviews will be marketed as if the product of spontaneous dialogue.[16] Unfortunately, critics of Ellison's work are too often more than happy to participate in this charade in exchange for the interview. Ralph Ellison is rarely caught off guard.[17]

In writing about Ellison, one inevitably crosses paths with literary critics who have reified him and use his objectified status and *Invisible Man* as proof of black artistic possibility. He has become both a symbol of black intellectual excellence and the living embodiment of black humanity and racial equality. As a result, Ellison is often explained but rarely engaged.[18] His critics usually describe him and his work. Rarely do they assume the authority to engage in a critique of Ellison. To grasp this celebratory vein one need only read the treatment of Ellison in *Chant of Saints* or the special issue of the *Carleton Miscellany* dedicated to his life and work.[19] Concerning the academic criticism of Ellison, one critic wrote,

> It is fair to say, however, that very little of the academic critical discourse on *Invisible Man* is indispensable and that a great majority is canonical, in that it implicitly or explicitly examines the novel within the frameworks provided by Ellison. . . . It follows that most of this critical discourse is constructive, at least implicitly idealizing, and illustrative of the accuracy of John Bayley's observation that "the usual critical instinct is to show that the work under discussion is as coherent, as aware, as totally organized as the critic desires his own representation of it to be."[20]

At present there are only a few book-length studies of Ellison in print in English. Kevin McSweeney's *Invisible Man: Race and Identity*, Robert O'Meally's *The Craft of Ralph Ellison*, Alan Nadel's *Invisible Criticism*, and Mark Busby's *Ralph Ellison* provide insightful if not occasionally overly deferential readings of Ellison. These studies are among the very few places where Ellison's work is systematically discussed and subjected to learned critical literary assessments.[21]

There have been instances when Ellison's life and work were subjected to uncivil and ad hominem attacks by critics.[22] Such attacks were not infrequent during that period in Afro-American letters in which black critics advocated black nationalism and a black aesthetic. One black aesthetic critic wrote:

> What may have been incisive in 1959 is cliché in 1970. What may have been an instructive allusion to white writers in the Sixties is Tomism in the Seventies. The burden that Ellison's genius puts on his manhood (and what our racial needs required) was for him to have been a lion

sui generis, not an acquiescer posing as a tiger. Black literature deserved its own references, its own standards, its own rules. Not in an aberrant denial of *anything* that came from white American culture, valid or otherwise, but as conscious insistence on the creating of an African-American text that derived its *raison d'être* from an African-American truth that exists in spite of the fact that it has never, until very recently, had a real pervasive life in the world of literature. . . .

But the amplitudes of Ellison's literary references, ensconced as they were in his mainstream mentality, did not permit this sort of aggressive, Black literary independence. All of his validities in his essays, and, in effect, in *Invisible Man*, are based on a white substructure. His achievement in the novel should have rendered him free of such a disabling psychosis, however. He should have stood *against* white literary values, not *with* them, and like W. E. B. Du Bois in history, and Alain Locke in cultural art, have set his own standard for the Fifties and Sixties that would have made him valid for the Seventies as a thinker.[23]

Such cliché-ridden critiques of Ellison and his work were commonplace during the late 1960s and early 1970s. More often than not, they were of little lasting intellectual value to Ellison as a writer or to his reading audience. Yet such attacks were intellectually significant precisely because they conveyed the attitudes of an Afro-American intellectual milieu in which Ellison often found himself entangled.

In 1969 President Lyndon Johnson awarded Ellison the Medal of Freedom. In 1970 "the Minister of Cultural Affairs in France, André Malraux, Ellison's hero from the thirties, awarded him the Chevalier de l'Ordre des Arts et Lettres."[24] He has been awarded honorary degrees from Tuskegee, Rutgers, the University of Michigan, Williams, Harvard, and Wesleyan. Despite Ellison's enormous talents and the accomplishment of *Invisible Man*, it is rare for a fiction writer with only one published novel (and no short-story collections) to have received all of these awards.[25] Ellison's willingness to assume the air of a senior statesman of American letters and his fondness for being celebrated when coupled with the magnificent achievement of *Invisible Man* have been primarily responsible for his phenomenal stature in American arts and letters.

Why Ellison has not published more remains a baffling question. The novel he is currently writing has been decades in the making. Like few other contemporary American novelists, Ellison must feel burdened after having reached the literary summit on the first try. It is an intimidating experience to live to see your first novel become a classic before you are able to publish your second. His already exacting standards when coupled with the burden of attempting to match or surpass *Invisible Man* have added to the difficulty of completing a second novel.[26] According to a friend who has read substantial portions of the unfinished second novel, "Ralph is insanely ambitious. He actually writes quickly, but won't release this book until he is sure that it is the greatest American novel ever written."[27] Friends, enemies, admirers, and critics who await this second Ellison novel are legion, leading literary critic Nathan Scott to observe that "his next book is one than which no other unbegotten novel had been more eagerly awaited in our time."[28]

Because of the prolific output of many of his contemporaries and his decreasing public recognition as an active writer, Ellison's delay in publishing a second novel suggests a rather extraordinary if not potentially self-destructive bid for excellence. Ellison could have long ago published whatever he had written. But the self-consciously artistic black intellectual is not merely a storyteller with a command of colorful and rich language but a student of Western culture, comparative Western literature, literary criticism, and literary theory. Ellison believes that the writing of one great masterpiece is far more significant than the writing of several good novels.

Ellison has attempted to teach black intellectuals that the entire tradition of Western literature and thought is theirs to appropriate. Such appropriations, according to Ellison, do not necessarily lead to the disvaluing of their own culture and people. Only by committing themselves to mastering the various artistic crafts of Western and neo-Western art can black American intellectuals and artists, in Ellison's eyes, provide the Afro-American folk culture with a fully developed and sophisticated fine artistic voice.[29]

My concern is with Ellison's unique bid for an ethnically marginal self-definition. A literary dialogue with *Invisible Man* is not pertinent to my study. Furthermore, I claim no expertise in such matters. Instead I am concerned with Ellison's views on American society, Afro-American culture, the political situation of black Americans, and the black writer's relationship to the other three. I want to understand the unique way that Ellison has confronted the victim status.

Analyzing Ellison in this way is particularly difficult, for like many creative writers, he is not a systematic sociopolitical thinker. At one moment Ellison might think a certain way, and shortly thereafter he might completely reverse his opinion. The problem is not that Ellison changes his mind but that he makes no effort to mention the contrasting view he held before or to account for the change. This eclecticism does not mark all of Ellison's discussions. There are some constant themes that he has been advocating or denouncing over the years. Few contemporary black intellectuals have created as highly developed a paratheoretical approach to Afro-American culture and identity as Ellison.[30] His cultural conceptions have extensive political ramifications that offset his attempt at forging an apolitical public intellectual persona.

Insofar as Ralph Ellison is and claims to be primarily a writer of fiction, by analyzing his political views I am in some respects isolating a segment of Ellison's enterprise that is marginal to his life's calling. I am unaware of any interview with Ellison in which he has sought or claimed the mantle of a political thinker. Ellison is not a creative political thinker, but he remains politically significant because of the political implications of his creative cultural views.

THE BIOGRAPHICAL BACKGROUND

Ralph Ellison was born in Oklahoma City, Oklahoma, on March 1, 1914. His southern-born parents, Lewis and Ida Milsap Ellison, had migrated to Oklahoma in search of racial freedoms that could not be found in the states of the former Confederacy.[31] Oklahoma had entered the union in 1907, a fact that explains its frontier character during Ellison's youth. Oklahoma was a frontier in three senses: it had been a refuge for blacks seeking to escape the Deep South; it had long been attractive to white migrants seeking a new beginning; and it housed a substantial Native American population. Though Oklahoma was segregated during Ellison's childhood, the frontier culture had offered black Oklahomans a sense of possibility.[32]

This sense of black possibility should not be overstated. When Ellison was seven, whatever lingering black popular belief there was in Oklahoma as a land of opportunity for blacks was either shattered or abruptly suspended. For generations of black Oklahomans, the spring of 1921 would be remembered for the Tulsa race riot. The viciousness and comprehensiveness of the white assault on the black residents and neighborhood of Tulsa far surpassed any similar single attack on blacks in the Deep South during the twentieth century. The entire black neighborhood in Tulsa was physically demolished. As many as three hundred blacks may have been killed. Over a thousand homes were destroyed.[33] Tulsa was a metaphor for the "southernness" of Oklahoma (in much the same way that the post–World War I race riots in Chicago and Detroit became metaphors for the "southernness" of those cities). The sense of possibility that inspired many blacks to venture to the Indian Territory was not subsequently reinforced by their daily lives once they had arrived. Yet, optimism among black Oklahomans regenerated in the aftermath of the Tulsa riot.[34]

When Ellison was three, his father died. Afterward Ralph, his brother Herbert, and his mother lived in relative poverty. Yet the upbringing that Ralph received from his mother transcended the boundaries of their immediate economic situation.[35] Though poor economically, Ralph was socialized into upwardly mobile, bourgeois visions and values. Describing the young Ellison's upbringing, Robert O'Meally wrote:

> Ralph and his younger brother Herbert were made to feel that the worlds of the rich and the white were approachable. This early confidence started off with Lewis Ellison, the avid reader who named his son after Emerson. It was reinforced by Ida Ellison, a determined woman, a stewardess in her church who valued action in *this* world. She brought home records, magazines, and books discarded in the white homes where she worked as a maid. And Mrs. Ellison saw to it that her sons had electric and chemistry sets, a roll-top desk and chair, and a toy typewriter. Her activism extended to politics. "If you young Negroes don't do something about things," she would tell Ralph and Herbert, "I don't know what's going to happen to this race." For her part, she was an ardent supporter of Eugene Debs' Socialist Party and canvassed for the party's gubernatorial candidate of 1914. In 1934

after Ralph had gone off to Tuskegee Institute, she was often jailed for attempting to rent buildings that Jim Crow laws had declared off limits to blacks.[36]

One imagines Ellison's mother as one of many black Americans who did not allow their sense of self to be determined by their racially constrained position within the economic order. During long periods of the twentieth century, black Ph.D.s carried luggage at Grand Central Station, while black college graduates loaded mail on U.S. postal trucks and waited on tables in swanky "white only" restaurants.[37] The story of the black window washer who wore a suit and tie to and from work only to change into and out of his cleaning clothes in the office bathroom is not just folklore. In these cases individuals were forced to develop a sense of their own value and dignity that did not rely on the status of the job they held. It is within this fluidity of black class and status perceptions that we can situate Lewis Ellison, seller of coal and ice and a former construction company foreman who worshiped the writings of Ralph Waldo Emerson.[38] From birth Ralph was exposed to the porous character of American class identities, having inherited in Oklahoma City the name of a Boston Brahmin. As a result, Ellison would never feel comfortable with one-dimensional, materialist conceptions of race and class.[39] In large measure this explains why Ellison would later never feel completely at home within the American Left.

As a child growing up in Oklahoma, Ellison was immersed in Afro-American folk culture. It was here, he informs us, that his love for the blues, jazz, and church music began. Musicians became idols. It was therefore not surprising that Ellison developed a fondness for the trumpet and became competent at classical music and jazz. The centrality of music in the young Ellison's life cannot be overstated. Oklahoma City was a critical place in the development of twentieth-century jazz,[40] a place where jazz musicians from all over the United States ventured in order to perfect their craft. Later they would journey to Kansas City and then perhaps on to New York. As a young man Ellison regularly attended the performances of the Blue Devils, the Oklahoma City-based jazz band that included such future jazz greats as Buster Smith, Oran "Hot Lips" Page, Walter Page, Lester Young, and Eddie Durham. They were the nucleus of the Benny Moten band and upon Moten's sudden death became a central component of Count Basie's orchestra.[41] Basie later added to the band fellow Oklahoma City resident and Ellison hero, vocalist "Little" Jimmy Rushing. As a young man Ellison would sit atop a neighborhood hill to listen to Rushing's voice bellowing out of dance halls blocks away.[42] Oklahoma City would also produce Charlie Christian, the jazz guitarist, who later gained fame with the Benny Goodman Orchestra. Music was vital to black life in Oklahoma City.

The young Ellison acquired formal musical training playing the trumpet in his high school band. He taught himself to play the ebullient music of Louis Armstrong. For a while Ellison received private lessons from the conductor of the Oklahoma City Orchestra in return for cutting his grass.[43]

In 1933 the young musician left Oklahoma City for Tuskegee Institute in Tuskegee, Alabama. Having won a music scholarship that did not include the cost of transportation to Tuskegee, Ellison undertook an apprenticeship with a well-known Oklahoma City hobo and rode the rails to Tuskegee.[44] This bold venture shows the intensity of the young Ellison's desire to obtain a college education and manifests a well-developed self-confidence. Not without his close calls, Ellison rode the rails through Alabama in 1933 fully aware of the case of the Scottsboro Boys two years earlier.

Ellison majored in music and music theory at Tuskegee in hopes of one day being able to write a symphony that would capture the blues in a classical form.[45] He had come to Tuskegee to study under William L. Dawson, a composer who Ellison would later claim (in 1964) "was, and probably still is the greatest classical musician in that part of the country."[46]

Ellison's experiences in the South would have a lifelong impact on his writing and beliefs concerning the American racial situation. It was in Alabama that Ellison first witnessed the severity of the race problem. He claims to have learned how to cope with southern racial etiquette in such a manner so as to not undermine his sense of self.

> I learned to outmaneuver those who interpreted my silence as submission, my efforts at self control as my fear, my contempt as awe before superior status, my dreams of faraway places and room at the top of the heap as defeat before the barriers of their stifling, provincial

world. And my struggle became a desperate battle which was usually fought, though not always, in silence; a guerrilla action in a larger war in which I found some of the most treacherous assaults against me committed by those who regarded themselves either as neutrals, as sympathizers, or as disinterested military advisors.[47]

Whether or not these statements accurately reflect Ellison's temper during his student days in Alabama is anyone's guess. Moreover, it is perhaps less important than the fact that Ellison wanted us to imagine his 1930's student days in that light when he composed the above essay in the early 1960s. It is highly probable that Ellison's sense of racial self-identity was securely intact prior to his journey to Tuskegee. If so, he would have certainly had a non-Alabaman black racial consciousness. After all, Ellison was from "the territory."[48] Yet to use his Oklahoman origins as the basis for explaining his response to southern racial etiquette would ultimately deny the point Ellison was trying to establish. Ellison wanted to posit his victorious Tuskegee confrontation with southern racial mores as proof of the ability of individuals to transcend their social condition.

Any attempt to understand Ellison's social thought must grasp his emphasis upon the limited ability of social/material environments to determine individual consciousness. A question remains. Would Ellison have been able to outmaneuver southern racial etiquette in Tuskegee had he been born and raised in Alabama? Ellison may have been on sturdier ground had he claimed Oklahoma City as the site where he learned to outmaneuver southern racial mores.

It is significant that Ellison chose to attend Tuskegee Institute. The institute during the period of Ellison's enrollment was not the Tuskegee of Booker T. Washington's days. During the decade prior to Ellison's attendance, Tuskegee had acquired a liberal arts emphasis as opposed to its earlier stress on industrial arts.[49] Yet Tuskegee's traditional upward mobility ethos remained, and it attracted the young Ellison, who shared with its founder an abiding faith in American possibility. At Tuskegee, Ellison found a few exceptional blacks who justified and sustained his belief in black possibility. Not only did Ellison work under William Dawson, but he was introduced to the formal study of literature by the chairman of the English department, Morteza Drexel Sprague. Sprague, who had been educated at Hamilton College, Harvard University, and

Columbia University, was, according to Albert Murray, the embodiment of the post–Booker T. Washington liberal arts emphasis at Tuskegee.[50] Under Sprague's tutoring Ellison studied Shakespeare, Eliot, Pound, Gertrude Stein, and Hemingway. It seems somewhat incongruous that in Alabama during the early 1930s, when lynchings were no rare occurrence and racial terrorism was institutionalized, black students were nestled in library chairs reading "The Waste Land." Such ironies are, for Ellison, everyday human phenomena that nurture the complexities of black life, complexities that many do not perceive, refuse to acknowledge, or erroneously perceive as insignificant.

Due to an administrative mix-up about his scholarship Ellison found himself without the necessary tuition and living fees for his senior year.[51] Ellison traveled to New York in the summer of 1936 hoping to earn enough money as a musician to pay for his last year at Tuskegee. He claims to have had little idea when he left school that he would never return. To migrating blacks, Harlem, the capital of black America, offered an image of unbounded freedom and opportunity. Like many other blacks who had ventured from the South to the great metropolis during the 1930s, Ellison discovered that opportunities were not ever-present. Unable to support himself as a musician, living on odd jobs and at times hand to mouth, Ellison sometimes slept outdoors on park benches.[52] During this period he did not think of himself as a writer but was flirting with the possibility of becoming a sculptor. In this endeavor he received encouragement from Alain Locke and studied with the black sculptor Richmond Barthe.[53] After a year of such study the aspirant sculptor quit.

Despite economic hardship in New York, Ellison was artistically rejuvenated by his exposure to jazz musicians and the music that he had idolized since his youth. While traveling in black artistic/literary circles Ellison met Langston Hughes and, later, Richard Wright.[54] In Hughes, Ellison found an ambivalent supporter.[55] In Wright, he found a temporary mentor. At the time of his initial meeting with Wright, Ellison still considered himself a musician. Yet he was able to substantively interact intellectually with Wright because of his broad familiarity with literature that had been nurtured at Tuskegee. Ellison described his initial meeting with Wright in a 1976 interview:

One of my early experiences with Dick Wright involved such an underestimation, with him assuming that I hadn't read many books [with] which I was, in fact, quite familiar. . . . He assumed that I hadn't read any of Marx . . . Conrad . . . Dostoevsky . . . Hemingway—and so on. I was somewhat chagrined by his apparent condescension, but instead of casting him in the role of misunderstanding "father," I swallowed my pride and told myself, "Forget it, you know what you know; so now learn what he thinks in terms of his Marxism and the insights he's gained as a developed writer of fiction." And that was the way it went.[56]

In typical Ellison fashion these comments conflict with other statements he made about the initial meeting with Wright. In a 1961 interview Ellison had stated, in response to the question, "At that time [of their initial meeting] were you dissatisfied with the sort of work Wright was doing?"

ELLISON: Dissatisfied? I was too amazed with watching the process of creation. I didn't understand quite what was going on, but by this time I had talked with Wright a lot and he was very conscious of technique. He talked about it not in terms of mystification but as writing know-how. "You must read so-and-so," he'd say. "You have to go about learning to write consciously. People have talked about such and such a problem, and have written about it. You must learn how Conrad, Joyce, Dostoievsky get their effects. . . ." He guided me to Henry James and to Conrad's prefaces, that type of thing. Of course, I knew that my own feelings about the world [and] about life, were different, but this was not even a matter to question. Wright knew what he was about, what he wanted to do, while I hadn't even discovered myself. I knew only that what I would want to express would not be in imitation of his kind of things.

STERN: So what sort of thing did you feel Wright was not doing that you wanted to do?

ELLISON: Well, I don't suppose I judged. I am certain I did not judge in quite so conscious a way, but I think I felt more complexity in life, and my background made me aware of a larger area of possibility.

Knowing Wright himself and something of what he was doing increased that sense of the possible. Also, I think I was less interested in an ideological interpretation of Negro experience. . . . When I came to discover a little more about what I wanted to express I felt that Wright was overcommitted to ideology—even though I, too, wanted many of the same things for our people.[57]

EMERGING WITHIN AND WITHOUT THE LEFT

Ellison's ambivalence toward Wright in the above contrasting quotes may indicate a love-hate relationship.[58] It is not difficult to imagine that the young Ellison came to a realization very early in his encounter with Wright that his artistic ambitions and talents superseded those of Wright. Whether or not Ellison's assessments were correct is, for me, an open question and beside the point. True or false, Ellison's views would have had to remain closeted as long as he did not have a substantial body of his own creative work to substantiate these privately held beliefs concerning himself and Wright. To have severely criticized Wright prior to the publication of his own novel would have left Ellison vulnerable to accusations of jealousy and spite. Prior to the publication of *Invisible Man*, Wright could have easily assumed himself to be Ellison's intellectual and artistic superior, given the quality of attention being paid to him by the broader American intellectual community. Likewise it is easy to imagine that Wright mistakenly assumed that Ellison also shared in the belief that Wright was his artistic and intellectual superior. Wright might have cavalierly assumed that he was Ellison's mentor. It is equally plausible that Ellison defiantly refused to view himself as Wright's student, though he may have acted the part. Lying in wait, Ellison might well have seethed under the potentially humiliating lie that he was momentarily "forced" to live vis-à-vis Wright.[59] The publication of *Invisible Man* would be Ellison's first major public break from Wright and an articulation of his honest feelings concerning Wright's work.

On one hand Ellison wants to view Wright's achievements as significant, and yet he consciously does not want to inflate the accomplishments of Wright in a world that produces Hemingways and Faulkners. In many respects, Ellison owes to Wright some of his initial opportunities to develop as a writer. As a result of Wright's prodding and encouragement, Ellison wrote a book review that was published in the fall 1937 issue of *New Challenge*, a journal funded by the Communist Party.[60] Later Wright would coax Ellison into writing a short story for *New Challenge*. Though the collapse of the journal prevented the publication of Ellison's short story, the young musician was well on his way to becoming an ex-musician.[61]

In February 1937 Ellison's mother died in Dayton, Ohio. Not only was Ellison psychologically unprepared for this possibility, but he came to Dayton for the funeral financially destitute.[62] In Dayton he and his brother supposedly slept in a car at night and hunted quail to stay alive. At the age of twenty-three, having slid from the promising and secure life of a student to the status of a hand-to-mouth musician-writer who was unsuccessfully raising tuition money for a return to college, Ellison might have entertained doubts about his ability to succeed in life. The doubt and the sense of marking time were shattered by the death of his mother, and he decided to commit himself totally to learning the writer's craft. Amidst tragedy, Ellison refocused his life.[63] At this time Ellison acquired his first sustained literary "ancestor," Ernest Hemingway.[64] Though Ellison claims that Wright was not and had never been his *literary* mentor, Wright can best be described as an early *intellectual* mentor.

Returning to New York, Ellison, with Wright's aid, was able to obtain a job on the Federal Writers' Project.[65] The Federal Writers' Project was a crucial social marginality facilitator for many black writers, including Richard Wright, Willard Motley, and Sterling Brown. It gave these black writers the time and resources necessary to write. Ellison once stated, "Roosevelt . . . was the architect of the writers' projects . . . and that gave me a chance to be a writer. I first started writing under WPA—that is, I was able to give time to writing because I could do work for them and learn to do my own."[66] Economically stable, Ellison learned to write. He contributed several essays to the Writers' Project volume, *The Negro in New York*. Ellison also worked on a project compiling black folklore. Ellison's exposure to the richness and diversity of urban black folklore may have subsequently inspired his use of folklore in his fiction. The Writers' Project had not only rescued Ellison from poverty, but it also substantially increased Ellison's exposure to the richness of black life.[67]

According to O'Meally, Ellison left the Federal Writers' Project in 1942 in order to become an editor of the *Negro Quarterly*. Here he stayed until shortly before the journal folded a year later. The *Negro Quarterly* was edited by Angelo Herndon, who in the early 1930s had faced execution as a result of his activities as a Communist Party U.S.A. organizer in Atlanta. He had been charged under a provision in the Georgia law adopted from former slave codes of "inciting Negroes to insurrection."[68] Herndon, at the time of his editorial partnership with Ellison, was attempting to move away from Communism. Harold Cruse commented on the *Negro Quarterly* in *The Crisis of the Negro Intellectual.*

The editors managed to get out four issues, beginning with Spring, 1942, and ending with Winter–Spring 1943. . . . There was nothing at all distinguished about this publication beyond its unabashed Communist Negro-white unity editorial slant. Literally swamped as it was with white writers, it serves as an example of how Communist influence and Left literary values smother and choke black cultural expression. The fear of black cultural assertion is so strong in the white Left that every precaution must be taken to influence even the most feeble rise of cultural self-evaluation among Negroes. . . . *The Negro Quarterly* died after four issues because Communist Left literary and critical values cannot sustain a "Review of Negro Life and Culture" even when these values emerge from the Negro Left.[69]

Cruse failed to mention that Sterling Brown, Richard Wright, J. Saunders Redding, Owen Dodson, and E. Franklin Frazier as well as Ellison and Herndon had appeared in the journal.[70] Cruse, in effect, accuses these black intellectuals of being manipulated by a "white" ideology and its conniving proponents (read white intellectuals). He cannot imagine that black intellectuals might willingly celebrate racial integration. Furthermore, Cruse simply does not accept at face value black intellectuals whose commitment to an interracial vision of the world might have drawn them to the Left. Instead he sees an attraction to the Left as the mechanism by which black intellectuals were drawn away from their "natural" home, black nationalism. It is therefore curious that Ralph Ellison, the author that Cruse celebrates for having best tapped into black culture in *Invisible Man*, would probably not have sought a haven in anything other than an integrated magazine.[71] Furthermore, in the 1930s and 1940s the only intellectual circles and journals that were committed to the inclusion of blacks as writers and editors were Left-oriented. Though undoubtedly at times racistly paternalistic, the Left at least offered black authors a way into print. Mainstream intellectual journals of this period, more often than not, simply ignored black writers.

Ellison's relationship to the Left differed significantly from that of Richard Wright. Wright had in crucial respects been educated within intellectual circles affiliated with the Communist Party. The Left, and in particular the Communist Party, not only helped Wright to acquire the technical training of a writer through the John Reed clubs but was also crucial in helping Wright to obtain the discipline and ethos of the intellectual life.[72] Intellectuals affiliated with the party became Wright's support community. Insofar as membership in the Communist Party had nurtured Wright during his formative intellectual years and sustained his break from the "normal" trajectory of black upward mobility, his membership in the party functioned as a social marginality facilitator.

Ellison did not seek an education from the Left. At the time of Wright's decision to introduce Ellison to Left political/intellectual circles, Ellison was one year short of completing college, a feat that was no everyday occurrence in the lives of blacks in 1936. Wright, we should remember, had not completed high school. Furthermore, Ellison had acquired intellectual/artistic discipline from the years spent attempting to master a musical idiom. Ellison did not desire to commit himself to membership in the organized Left, and yet he needed the Left to sustain his early interests in writing at least by the support and catharsis he received through being published. Regardless of the intentions of the Left, Ellison and other black writers used the opportunity made available to them.[73]

Ellison devised a rather atypical strategy for announcing to the Left that he was not truly at home in leftist circles. Unlike other writers, black and white, who would donate their work to the party's organs and other progressive journals, Ellison demanded payment for his work. He would not donate his writings to "the cause" precisely because he wanted it to be known that he was not completely committed to it.[74]

Furthermore, Ellison by his very nature was not the political man that Wright was. Wright lived for politics in much the same way that Ellison lived for culture. Consequently, the internal machinations of the organized political Left with its intrigue, passionate discourse, political activism, exaggerated sense of self-importance, and reinforcement of a sense of being an outsider were far more attractive to Wright than to Ellison.[75] Unlike Wright, Ellison did not desire to use the Left as a social marginality facilitator. Insofar as membership in the Left gave boundaries to Wright's "outsider" status, Ellison was engaged in guerrilla warfare. While Wright always viewed himself as an outsider and desired to live and write as one, Ellison did not view his artistic calling as making white America conscious of the outsider status of blacks.[76] Instead, Ellison desired to make America conscious of the utter centrality of black culture to American culture.[77]

Yet Ellison entered the Left's intellectual circles as an unknown entity with no "calling cards" and few "connections." Larry Neal noted:

The Left wing, particularly the Communist Party, represented *one of the main means by which a young Black writer could get published.* There were perhaps other routes through the Establishment. But for a young Black writer checking out the literary happenings in 1937 (Ellison was about 28 years old when he wrote his first piece for Challenge, a Black left-oriented magazine), the Party was very attractive. After all, was not Richard Wright on that side of the street? And did not the Communist Party seem very amenable to young Black talent? . . .

Never having been a hard-core ideologue in the first place, Ellison appears to have been exceedingly uncomfortable as a leftist polemicist. . . . You can perceive another kind of spirit trying to cut through the Marxist phrase-mongering, another kind of spirit trying to develop a less simplistic, more viable attitude towards not only the usable content of Afro-American culture in America, but more importantly, a sense of the *meaning* of that culture's presence and its manifestations as they impinged upon "white culture". One isolatable political tendency that begins to emerge at the end of Ellison's Marxist period is a nascent, loosely structured form of Black Nationalism.[78]

Though essentially correct in echoing Ellison's recent statements, Neal underemphasizes the role of Richard Wright in Ellison's early career. It was not merely that Wright was a Communist too. Except perhaps for Langston Hughes, Wright was *the* black communist writer of his day. His valued status as a writer not only allowed him to encourage Ellison to write but gave him the personal connections to midwife Ellison's writings into print. Through Wright, Ellison met prominent white intellectuals (Granville Hicks, Clifford Odets, and Malcolm Cowley). Ellison soon became a welcomed presence within black leftist intellectual circles in Harlem. In his study of the Communist Party in Harlem during the depression, Mark Naison wrote,

> An extraordinary number of black intellectuals and creative artists gravitated toward Party circles in Harlem, as members, as fellow travelers, or as participants in discussions or social events. "Richard Wright was in the WPA," Louise Thompson recalls: "We used to have discussions in our home with him, Paul Robeson, Langston [Hughes] and Jacques Romain, a Haitian poet we greatly admired. We had jam sessions, long discussions. . . . Ralph Ellison used to be part of that scene as well. He used to be at my home almost every day." Abner Berry recalled discussing "Proust, Joyce, Dostoyevsky, and the role of symbolism in literature" with Wright, Ellison, and Theodore Ward.[79]

Between 1937 and 1944 Ellison contributed over twenty book reviews to various leftist journals, including *New Challenge*, *Direction*, *Negro Quarterly*, and the *New Masses*. During this period Ellison appears to have adhered to the Communist Party's "Negro Nation" thesis. Developed by black Communist Party theoretician Harry Haywood (see Haywood's classic statement, *Negro Liberation*), the Negro Nation thesis viewed black Americans, then residing disproportionately in a southern "black belt," as constituting a nation within a nation. It was the duty of black writers to help awaken the consciousness of blacks to their national and class oppressions. By aligning themselves with workers of other nationalities, black workers could join a multiracial class struggle against their multiracial bourgeois oppressors.[80]

Ellison's earliest forays into print were patterned after the guidelines issued by Wright in his "Blueprint for Negro Literature." Yet amidst the production of left-wing dogma, Ellison sought a personal voice. Increasingly ill at ease with portrayals of blacks as reactive subjects to oppression, Ellison by 1940 had recognized that his vision of fiction differed from that of Wright and other social realists. "His concern with style, with folklore, and with history as a 'repository of values' eclipsed his enchantment with black proletarians, scarred, battered and on the run."[81]

In *After Alienation: American Novelists in Mid-Century*, Marcus Klein discusses the peculiar importance of an editorial penned by Ellison in 1943.[82] The unsigned editorial comment that appeared in the *Negro Quarterly* indicated a break with the economic Marxism that Ellison had been generally espousing up to that point. Challenging black political leadership, the young Ellison wrote,

> A third major problem, and one that is indispensable to the centralization and direction of power, is that of learning the meaning of the myths and symbols which abound among the Negro masses. For without this knowledge, leadership, no matter how correct its program, will fail. Much in Negro life remains a mystery; perhaps the zoot suit conceals profound political meaning; perhaps the symmetrical frenzy of the Lindy-hop conceals clues to great potential powers— if only Negro leaders would solve this riddle. On this knowledge depends the effectiveness of any slogan or tactic. . . . The problem is psychological; it will be solved only by a Negro leadership that is aware of the psychological attitudes and incipient forms of action which the black masses reveal in their emotion-charged myths, symbols, and war-time folklore. Only through a skillful and wise manipulation of these centers of repressed social energy will Negro resentment, self-pity and the indignation be channelized to cut through temporary issues and become transformed into positive action.[83]

During the middle 1940s Ellison became thoroughly disillusioned with American Communism. Though never a party member, Ellison seems to have rejected Communist Party circles because of the opportunism they displayed in reference to black America.[84] Since that time his politics have gradually become more and more establishmentarian. One of the enduring legacies of Ellison and his generation of former American leftists who came of political age during the 1930s and 1940s is that their abhorrence of the vulgarities present in real world Communism (for example, Stalin's Soviet Union) often generated the rejection of socialism as a normative political vision. In leaving Communism, Ellison reemerges twenty years later as an American patriot. In many respects Ellison's politics are but reflections of his aesthetic and cultural views that had never been attuned to leftist thought.[85] Ellison is, after all, a meritocratic elitist, cultural pluralist. He believes that it is the duty of the writer to provide the folk with values by which to live. It is not the duty of the writer to provide the folk with governance. That is someone else's task. Those trained to perform it will be better at it than the writer. Ellison's elitism respects specialization and a division of labor.

It was, therefore, not surprising that Ellison disagreed with poet Robert Lowell's decision to write a letter to the press refusing to participate in the White House Art Festival in 1965 on the grounds that his presence there might be viewed as support for Johnson's foreign policy in Southeast Asia.[86] Ellison, who gladly attended the event, later commented on Lowell's actions.

I do not think it was necessary. When Lowell wrote to the President—and it was a skillfully written letter—he stated his motives of conscience, his fear that his presence would commit him to the President's foreign policy.

In other words, he feared the potency of his own presence in such a setting, a potency which would seem to rest in his person rather than in the poetry for which we praise him and consider him great. But, he didn't stop there, the letter got to the press, and once this happened, it became a political act, a political gesture.

I think this was unfortunate. The President wasn't telling Lowell how to write his poetry, and I don't think he's in any position to tell the President how to run the government. . . .

Actually, no one was questioned as to his attitudes, political or otherwise—except by Dwight Macdonald. It wasn't that kind of occasion. Any and every opinion was represented there. Millard Lampell, who had been picketing the White House, had part of his play presented, and his background is no secret. So it was not in itself a political occasion, and all of the hullabaloo was beside the point. I was very much amazed, having gone through the political madness that marked the intellectual experience of the "thirties," to see so many of our leading American intellectuals, poets, novelists—free creative minds— once again running in a herd. One may take a personal position concerning a public issue which is broader than his personal morality, and the others make a herd of free creative minds! Some of my best friends are mixed up in it—which leaves me all the more amazed.[87]

Ellison's statement that the dissent against the United States foreign policy in Vietnam was reminiscent of the madness of the 1930s was revealing precisely because it was such an obviously forced comparison. Besides the intense disagreements within the intelligentsia over the Vietnam question, the 1930s did not witness an American military onslaught on foreign peoples. What remains surprising about Ellison's response to Lowell are his rather blatantly antidemocratic views. One wants to ask Ellison why Lowell does not have the right (or duty) to express his political opinions to the president. Is this, as Ellison has so often informed us, a nation predicated upon democratic ideals?[88] Ellison's disrespect for Lowell's desire to participate in governance is linked to his antiliberal conception of democracy and ultimately to his perception of the ideal writer as politically disengaged.

In large measure Ellison was angry at Lowell precisely because he did not agree with Lowell's position on the Vietnam War. In an uncharacteristically uncritical article, Richard Kostelanetz celebrated as an act of bravery Ellison's moral parochialism on the Vietnam War. The sentiments conveyed to Kostelanetz were also responsible for Ellison's distaste for Martin Luther King's criticism of Johnson's war policy.

Ellison insists that Negro Americans should keep their eyes fixed on the classic goals—integration, cultural autonomy, freedom of movement, equal opportunity, and a share of political power. Now that these goals are within realization, he fears that various distractions may sabotage the effort. Similarly, it takes genuine courage for a writer to go against the majority opinion of his own profession, but this is precisely the personal strength which Ellison consistently displays, as in publicly defending American involvement in Vietnam, less out of patriotic enthusiasm than tragic necessity. "I don't see us withdrawing from the war," he said, for once looking out the window and then back at me. "We have certain responsibilities to the Vietnamese and the structure of power in the world. It's too bad, but that's the way it is."[89]

It is significant that Ellison invoked a realpolitik argument against black American criticism of American involvement in the Vietnam War. While his belief that blacks should close ranks with the pro–civil rights administration of Lyndon Johnson is understandable on pragmatic political grounds, it is a line of argument that implies that black Americans had ethnic allegiances that transcended their national allegiances. It was characteristically un-Ellisonian to suggest that black Americans, in order to obtain full citizenship rights, had to relinquish the moral prerogatives of American citizenship (that is, criticism of American foreign policy). The argument so thoroughly diverges from Ellison's cultural interpretation of blacks as "omni-Americans" that one senses that Ellison's ultimate motives center around his support of the war effort. Some might interpret Ellison's position as quasi–black nationalist, but even this would be a problematic interpretation given the large numbers of blacks who were dying in Vietnam.

By mid-1950 Ellison had emerged as a liberal establishmentarian elitist who proclaimed the virtues of high culture artistic disengagement.[90] In his technocratic view of democratic politics there was little room for the actively involved, humanistic artist. He has stated, "When writers write about politics, usually they are wrong. The novel at its best demands a sort of complexity of vision which politics doesn't like. Politics has as its goal the exercise of power—political power—and it isn't particularly interested in truth in the way that the novel form demands that the novelist must be."[91] One wants to ask Ellison who is usually "correct" when they write about politics? Ellison's view of the world renders everyone and everything overtly specialized and narrow. One wonders on what basis community life can exist. His advice to the would-be artist—as social critic—is to leave politics to the politicians and art to the artists. Besides, politics is a passing phenomenon; art endures.

Ellison's rejection of the Left signaled his rejection of activist politics. Yet it is often forgotten that Ellison's involvement with the Left had been his only real flirtation with activist politics.[92] Once his dependency on the Left declined, a phenomenon that occurred gradually as Ellison continued to publish and broaden his intellectual circles, Ellison discarded the activist Left, particularly the Communist Party. Ellison was far too serious to mistake the ideologues around the Community Party for creative intellectual confreres. Moreover, after the publication of *Invisible Man*, Ellison also retreated from perfunctory social encounters with the left-wing Harlem literati, including Langston Hughes. Hughes came to symbolize for Ellison the life and mind of a frivolous and/or artistically unambitious black intellectual.[93]

Marxism had historically functioned as a democratic mode of discourse for parochial American intellectuals seeking entrance into cosmopolitan American intellectual circles.[94] As a common vernacular it could be studied and mastered by almost anyone who took time to do so. As such it was the intellectual midwife to numerous American intellectuals from the periphery (the South, a small town, or within ethnic parochialism). Blacks were no exception. Marxism provided many intellectuals with a "culture of common discourse" (borrowed from Gouldner's "culture of critical discourse").[95] In part, the accessibility of the culture of common discourse is responsible for the Left having historically functioned as one of the most pluralistic and racially open-ended intellectual subcultures within the American intelligentsia.

Like many American intellectuals, Ralph Ellison used this culture of common discourse as a guidepost for his early travels within the New York intellectual scene. Ellison, the migrant from Oklahoma by way of Alabama, used this intellectual gateway even though he was not committed to activist leftist politics. This behavior was not uncommon. Many liberals and even some conservatives from the American hinterland have used the Left to manage their intellectual introduction into the overbearing world of the metropolis. Having acquired a sufficient degree of security (financially, artistically, and psychologically), they leave the Left and pursue their artistic desires. Such behavior is often manifested in intellectuals who claim to have rejected the Left for political reasons but who in fact rejected the Left to get out of active political involvement altogether. Such is the case with Ralph Ellison.

In claiming that Ellison left the politically engaged or activist Left, I in no way want to claim that Ellison rejected leftist political ideals and circles entirely. After the publication of *Invisible Man*, Ellison became a familiar fixture within the anti-Stalinist, liberal left wing of the New York literary community.[96] While polemical debates raged in these circles, their tone and quality were quite different from those that engulfed the circles Ellison had previously inhabited. In his discussion of the history of the New York Jewish intellectual community (the "New York Intellectuals") that came of age during the middle and late 1930s, Daniel Bell labels Ellison a "Gentile Cousin."[97] In *Making It*, Norman Podhoretz refers to Ellison as a "kissing cousin."[98] Interestingly, the only other black intellectual referred to as a cousin or relative by Bell and Podhoretz is James Baldwin.

From his earliest days as a conscious artist, Ellison probably entertained some views of art that conflicted with the prevailing Marxist dogma as espoused by the Communist Party U.S.A.[99] As Ellison matured artistically, he became increasingly hostile to Marxism. A novice writer trying to use the Left as a creative way station, Ellison tactically chose not to reveal the infant kernels of his anti-Marxist aesthetics. After all, the Communist Party U.S.A. demanded intellectual conformity. However cosmopolitan the Left was in allowing a variety of people to participate in its various debates, it was parochial about the variety of debates it tolerated. One debate that was not easily tolerated in Communist Party circles centered around black culture as a source of political opposition.[100] Discussions of Afro-American culture as the site of political opposition were apparently dogmatically condemned as "bourgeois nationalism." The black freedom struggle was seen as one component of the American class struggle. In order to maintain the belief that the idea of blacks as proletarians was more significant than the idea of blacks as blacks, the Communist Party dictates demanded the repression of arguments that found virtue or significance in cultural distinctiveness among the American proletariat. Ellison must have certainly viewed this attempt to level culturally all proletarians, including blacks, as not only a violation of his reality but simpleminded.

Though Ellison used the Left to gain access to literary journals and New York intellectual circles, he did not need the Left to provide him with access to intellectual discipline or an intellectual tradition. Unlike most other black writers, Ellison was raised within a black intellectual/artistic tradition.[101] As a young man Ellison acquired the discipline of the musician and the ambitions of the composer. As such, Ellison never quite experienced that jolting, disorientating moment many black intellectuals experience when they reject the pursuit of social and economic mobility for nascent intellectual/artistic ambitions. Ellison had attended college in order to become a musician. Insofar as the blues, gospel, and jazz were an everyday part of Ellison's youth and the cornerstones of an Afro-American artistic/intellectual tradition, Ellison has always viewed the desire to become a writer as ethnically black. That is, Ellison did not have to violate ethnic boundaries in deciding to become a novelist. The fact that Ellison's intellectual development occurred through the very center of Afro-American artistic/intellectual traditions helps to explain why he, unlike Richard Wright or Amiri Baraka, probably never felt the need to divorce himself from Afro-American culture when seeking a creative space. Instead of retreating to the margins of Afro-American ethnicity, Ellison believed that he could intellectually prosper from its cultural center. Ellison would attempt to harness literarily the traditions he knew best. More precisely, Ellison would attempt to capture the blues in literary form.

THE EMERGENCE OF A BLUES ONTOLOGY

According to many literary critics, Ellison's efforts to capture the blues literarily were realized in *Invisible Man*. Albert Murray, a prominent Afro-American man of letters and Ellisonian kindred spirit states,

> *Invisible Man* was par excellence the literary extension of the blues. It was as if Ellison had taken an everyday twelve bar blues tune . . . and

scored it for an orchestra. . . .

It was a first rate novel, a blues odyssey, a tall tale about the fantastic misadventures of one American Negro, and at the same time a proto-typical story about being not only a twentieth century American but also a twentieth century man, the Negro's obvious predicament sym-bolizing everybody's essential predicament. And like the blues, and echoing the irrepressibility of America itself, it ended on a note of promise, ironic and ambiguous perhaps, but a note of promise still. The blues with no aid from existentialism have always known that there was no clear-cut solutions for the human situation.[1]

The significance of the blues for Ellison extends far beyond the music's literary uses. Ellison perceived in and acquired from the blues an ontol-ogy, a philosophy of life that permeated his entire way of looking at politics and society. The origins of Ellison's drift away from economic Marxism lay in his recognition and acceptance of the blues as a metaphor for human existence. Once acquired, Ellison's blues-oriented philoso-phy of life allowed him to generate a sustained and utterly devastating attack not only on black protest fiction but also on the nonfiction pro-test writings of black social scientists and their white colleagues, par-ticularly as they pertained to the study of the Negro. More importantly, the blues ontology as a philosophy of life grounded Ellison in an ap-proach to the artistic quest that generated and sustained intellectual dis-cipline and artistic ambitions far beyond those that normally emerged within Ellison's intellectual milieu. This was particularly true during those torturous years when the young Ellison was writing *Invisible Man.*

In "Richard Wright's Blues," an essay published in 1945, Ellison of-fered a seminal definition of the blues.

The blues is an impulse to keep the painful details and episodes of a brutal experience alive in one's aching consciousness, to finger its jagged edge and to transcend it, not by the consolation of philosophy but by squeezing from it a near-tragic, near-comic lyricism. As a form, the blues is an autobiographical chronicle of personal catastrophe expressed lyrically. . . .

. . . Their attraction lies in this, that they at once express both the agony of life and the possibility of conquering it through sheer toughness of spirit. They fall short of tragedy only in that they provide no solution, offer no scapegoat but the self.[2]

Elaborating on Ellison's definition, Albert Murray later wrote,

In a sense the whole point of the blues idiom lyric is to state the facts of life. Not unlike ancient tragedy, it would have the people for whom it is composed and performed confront, acknowledge, and proceed in spite of, and even in terms of, the ugliness and meanness inherent in the human condition. It is thus a device for making the best of a bad situation.

Not by rendering capitulation tolerable, however, and certainly not by consoling those who would compromise their integrity, but—in its orientation to continuity in the face of adversity and absurdity. . . .

. . . There is also the candid acknowledgement and sober acceptance of adversity as an inescapable condition of human existence—and perhaps in consequence an affirmation disposition towards all obstacles.[3]

For Ellison and Albert Murray, the blues contained an indigenously American form of existentialism.[4] Ellison had been introduced to existentialism through his reading of André Malraux's *Man's Hope*.[5] In that novel Miguel de Unamuno, the Spanish existentialist philosopher, appears as a character. During the late 1930s, at the height of the Spanish civil war, Ellison and Richard Wright met often to discuss Unamuno's *The Tragic Sense of Life*. Concerning this period Ellison has stated that his reading of Unamuno was not only an intellectually exciting event but made him aware of the existential elements in black spirituals and the blues.[6] Concerned with developing a means of reconciling individual freedom with social determinism, Ellison found himself in pursuit of a Marxist-Freudian synthesis. Existentialism seemed to offer a way out. In reaction to the prevailing economic Marxism of his early days in New York, Ellison ultimately became more concerned with recuperating the autonomous individual from complete social determinism. He became obsessed with the issue of individual freedom.

Much like the early Sartre's ideas in *Being and Nothingness*, Ellison's blues ontology gave rise to a notion of freedom void of historical contexts. This notion of freedom assumed that regardless of social conditions and circumstances, the individual would still have to make choices governing his or her life. In making these choices the individual either successfully or unsuccessfully realized his or her freedom. Whether one was wealthy or homeless, these choices would have to be made.

The young Sartre had written, "No factual state whatever it may be (the political and economic structure of society, the psychological 'state', etc.) is capable by itself of motivating any act whatsoever. . . . No factual state can determine consciousness to apprehend it as a negative or as a lack."[7] In his history of existential Marxism in postwar France, Mark Poster elaborated upon the early Sartre's notion of freedom.

Determinism in any form, whether as the "economic base" of official Marxism or as the libido of orthodox Freudians, was not an explanation of action to Sartre, because it was always the individual who had to choose the course of action and prior to that the meaning of the situation. Reality must first be interpreted, must be given value, must be organized into an intelligible totality and must be made the object of an intention, before action was possible. Since *"freedom is originally a relation to the given"* both the given and freedom, the outside and the inside, society and the individual were in a reciprocal, mutually reinforcing dialectical tension, in which neither could overcome or "determine" the other.[8]

The relationship between the individual and the given is reminiscent of what Murray and Ellison refer to as "antagonistic cooperation." In *The Hero and the Blues*, Murray wrote:

Promising young men in stories, as in life, do not become heroes by simply keeping their police records clean and their grade point averages high enough to qualify them for status jobs and good addresses inside the castle walls. . . . Those young men who become heroes whose deeds merit statues, red-letter days and epics do so by confronting and slaying dragons. . . . The sinister circumstances . . . *cooperate* with the hero by virtue of the very fact of and nature of their existence. They help beget real-life and storybook heroes alike, not only by generating the necessity for heroism in the first place but also by contesting its development at every stage and by furnishing the occasion for its fulfillment. . . . The degree of cooperation is always equal to the amount of antagonism.[9]

In his effort to reject the protest literary practice of depicting blacks as all-encompassing sufferers, Ellison rejected social deterministic theories. As such, *Invisible Man* stands as the major critique of Wright's *Black Boy* and *Native Son*. Yet in searching for and finally arriving at a space that allowed the articulation of individual black wills, Ellison slowly crept too deeply into the quagmire of bourgeois liberty.

Ellison's emphasis on the irrepressibility of individual freedom essentially led him into a cul de sac from which the utter viciousness of racism and capitalism could not be comprehensively analyzed and attacked. Ellison simply could not reconcile the immense oppression of black America with his claims for healthy blues-oriented black cultural adaptations. Did not racial oppression have negative cultural repercussions for the oppressed?[10] Had Ellison been exposed to a more culturally enriched Marxism (such as that of Antonio Gramsci), perhaps he could have been able to reconcile the creative articulations of the will of oppressed blacks with the reproduction of their oppression and a recognition of the devastating impact of such oppression on their lives.[11] To deal with oppression humanely does not require denying the ramifications of oppression for the oppressed and the oppressor. Without a Gramscian type of framework Ellison's critique of deterministic discussions of oppression rings evasive. Ellison's arguments against Abram Kardiner and Lionel Ovesey's *The Mark of Oppression*, Gunnar Myrdal's *An American Dilemma*, or Daniel P. Moynihan's *The Negro Family: The Case for National Action* are insightful but remain one-dimensional proclamations of black human agency against one-dimensional social-scientific denials of such agency. An underdetermined conception of freedom is employed by Ellison in a critique of overdetermined conceptions of freedom's denial.

A major shortcoming of the Ellison-Murray formulation of the blues ontology lies precisely where fault was found with Sartre's early existentialist notion of freedom. Writing as a sympathetic critic of Sartre, Maurice Merleau-Ponty argued that Sartre's concept of freedom was too limited in contextualizing the subject. Merleau-Ponty noted that "if the slave displays freedom as much by living in fear as by breaking his chains, then it cannot be held that there is such a thing as free action."[12] We can easily perceive similar shortcoming in Ellison's notion of freedom, particularly in his discussion of the freedom experienced by Richard Wright in Mississippi.[13]

The blues hero must ultimately be able to "roll with the punches." After all, once one dragon is slain, others will inevitably appear. "Improvisation," Murray tells us "is the ultimate human (i.e. heroic) endowment."[14] The blues-oriented hero is a master of improvisation.

The dominant methodological approaches of the social sciences to the study of black Americans during the 1930s through the mid-1960s tended to view Afro-Americans as pathological to the extent that their behavior differed from mainstream white behavior.[15] Blacks were not viewed as a people engaged in affirmative cultural self-production. Ellison viewed such arguments as flawed precisely because they denied to black people the human attribute of improvisation, that is, a recognition of their willed attempt to humanize their environment however materialistically wretched it might have been.

As a young writer Ellison first systematically articulated his distaste for the social-scientific depiction of Afro-Americans in a review of Gunnar Myrdal's *An American Dilemma*.[16] Commissioned in 1944 by the *Antioch Review*, his review essay was subsequently rejected for publication. Twenty years later he included the review in *Shadow and Act*. Perhaps the *Antioch Review* did not appreciate the uncelebratory stance of Ellison's critique of American capitalist philanthropy's interest in the study of the Negro. Ellison argued that the Carnegie Corporation's study "is a blueprint for a more effective exploitation of the South's natural, industrial and human resources."[17] Yet, from our vantage point, the most significant charge leveled against Myrdal was that he viewed black-white relations through a white-centered, undialectical framework. Myrdal had created a world in which blacks were completely reactive to whites. The Swedish economist had written, "The Negro's entire life and, consequently, also his opinions on the Negro problem are, in the main, to be considered as secondary reactions to more primary pressures from the side of the dominant white majority."[18] Ellison replied: "But can a people (its faith in an idealized American Creed notwithstanding) live and develop for over three hundred years simply by *reacting*? Are American Negroes simply the creation of white men, or have they at least helped to create themselves out of what they found around them? Men have made a way of life in caves and upon cliffs, why cannot Negroes have made a life upon the horns of the white man's dilemma?"[19] Ellison accused Myrdal of seeing "Negro culture and personality as the product of a 'social pathology.' " Ellison not only rejects this view but labels as absurd Myrdal's call to black Americans to assimilate into American culture. What, Ellison asked, is Negro culture if it is not American? Furthermore, he questioned the degree to which an entity called American culture could ever be construed as simply the culture of whites. After all, blacks had informed this culture. Ellison is also incensed by Myrdal's intuitive racist assumptions that whites should innately function as the reference group for blacks. He rhetorically states that the simple fact that it is whites who participate in lynchings and are imprisoned in consumerism does not and should not inspire blacks to follow in their footsteps.

> What is needed in our country is not an exchange of pathologies, but a change of the basis of society. This is a job which both Negroes and whites must perform together. In Negro culture there is much of value for America as a whole. What is needed are Negroes to take it and create of it "the uncreated consciousness of their race." In doing so they will do far more, they'll help create a more human American.
>
> Certainly it would be unfair to expect Dr. Myrdal to see what Negro scholars and most American social scientists have failed to see.[20]

Ellison correctly noted that Myrdal's conception of black Americans did not include them being involved in willed self-creation. In denying creative black human agency, Myrdal silenced black heroic activity. But Ellison also recognized that Myrdal's white-centered analysis was not simply the result of his race or foreign nationality, for most significant black American social scientists of the day viewed black America through the same warped lens. Charles Valentine in *Culture and Poverty* would later label this type of white-centered analysis the "pejorative tradition" and would place the black sociologist E. Franklin Frazier in its very core.[21] In this sense, Frazier was to black social science what Richard Wright was to black fiction.

A quintessential social-scientific work in the pejorative tradition remains the classic 1951 study of the Negro's personality, *The Mark of Oppression*. The study concluded,

These people [black Americans] have no fantasy escape. Many of them cannot imagine anything much further than a middle-class home. Religion does not answer their needs, hence they are constant prey to new religious adventurers. We have seen little evidence of genuine religiosity among Negroes. They have invented no religion of their own. The one that comes closest to it, that of Father Divine, encourages a grotesque flight into unreality by the crude device of denying the real world and creating an artificial one.[22]

In response to such ridiculous but respected social-scientific claims concerning black Americans, Ellison wrote, "Prefabricated Negroes are sketched on sheets of paper and superimposed upon the Negro community; then when someone thrusts his head through the pages and yells, 'Watch out there, Jack, there's people living under here,' they are all shocked and indignant."[23]

Ellison also noted the extent to which Myrdal, Frazier, and numerous other social scientists were ignorant of the black contribution to the development of a pluralistic American national culture. Myrdal assumed that American culture was divorced from blacks and that black culture was non-American. Ellison viewed blacks as "omni-Americans," a concept expounded by Albert Murray. It is certain that Ellison's notion of the cultural pluralism of black and white Americans stemmed from his sense of the impact of blacks' cultural improvisation on their American environment.

Ellison's views of Afro-American culture as presented in the 1944 review of *An American Dilemma* would help to shape the texture of Afro-American literary and cultural studies for the next forty years. His explicit and well-reasoned defense of the whiteness of black Americans and the blackness of white Americans would fuel an intense anti-Ellisonian backlash during the 1960s. Ellison's unwillingness to denounce most things white, particularly his white ancestors, made Ellison a hated target among those who had clothed themselves in a parochial blackness. Ellison probably viewed such nationalist critics as Hoyt Fuller, LeRoi Jones (Imamu Amiri Baraka), Addison Gayle, and others who argued for a black cultural separatist tradition and a black aesthetic as distorters of a complex cultural reality.[24] For maintaining this position Ellison was thought by some to be an old-fashioned, reactionary black intellectual whose ideas were irrelevant to the struggle for black liberation.

Black cultural nationalists, however parochial, were not without grounds for some of their criticisms of Ellison. After all, Ellison was at the forefront of emphatically denying any significant Afro-American cultural connection with Africa. In discussing Africa with interviewer Harold Isaacs, Ellison appears dogmatic in his attempts to deny any American Negro cultural linkage to Africa and almost fanatical in proclaiming a lack of a personal interest in Africa and Africans.[25] Perhaps Ellison thought that an identification with Africa would be self-stigmatizing. Such internalized racist thoughts concerning Africa were frequently held by black intellectuals of his generation. On the other hand, Ellison's proclaimed disinterest in Africa may have been a knee-jerk response to the romanticization of Africa then taking place within some black intellectual circles. Interestingly, many commentators on Ellison have mistaken his defense of a distinct Afro-American culture as a defense of an African-influenced Afro-American culture.[26] In arguing that Afro-Americans were culturally created on the shores of America, Ellison sounds a great deal like E. Franklin Frazier, not Melville Herskovits.

Ellison at times seemed to ignore all nonwhite cultural influences on black Americans when discussing Afro-American cultural complexity. In his interviews and essays describing black culture, Ellison completely ignores the Hispanic-Afro-American cultural connection. Worse, having grown up in a former Indian territory where some Indians owned slaves, Ellison's neglect of the cultural exchanges between blacks and Native Americans is quite conspicuous. Equally conspicuous is Ellison's omission of the cultural connection between West Indians and indigenous black Americans. The cultural diversity of Afro-America was far more extensive than Ellison would have had us believe. Nevertheless, it was his willingness to identify cultural exchanges with white America as the primary influence on black American culture that generated much of the black nationalist antagonism toward him.

To the extent that Ellison endeavors to situate black life in the very core of American life, his project on some level is to make us conscious of black cultural richness and diversity. However, to the extent that Ellison circumscribes Afro-American life solely within American and Western cultures, he does not adequately confront the degree to which Afro-Americans are a pariah people. Because Ellison's scope is limited to American and Western cultural landscapes, he cannot accurately engage the degree to which blacks were not only created by Western discourses but created as outsiders. Ellison's vantage point precludes the development of an Afro-American critique of Western cultural hegemony and the cultural objectification of nonwhite "others." Equally important, Ellison cannot grasp that there might be self-definitions of the "others" that are not constructed by Western discourses. In fact, Ellison is so thoroughly circumscribed by a Western cultural myopia that he continually invokes the idea that the best Western art is "universal." Universal in whose eyes? In addition, he does not recognize that key defining moments of the West occurred when it confronted nonwesterners. As such, one cannot really speak of the West without invoking images of Africans and other "others."

When talking about the forces that went into creating a vibrant Afro-American culture, he omits in his descriptions discussions of the barbaric repression of black peoples and cultures that took place in Africa as well as on the shores of the New World. Did not this trauma and the dislocation of life significantly influence Afro-American identity and culture? What became of African cultures in the New World? In attempting to circumvent the immense power differentials between slave and slave master or oppressed blacks and freer whites, Ellison repeatedly provides us with claims about mutual cultural borrowing and enrichment between American blacks and whites. While the slaves certainly influenced the masters, their influences seem paltry when compared with the ways that the masters culturally influenced the slaves. Ellison would have us believe that this moment of extraordinary repression and exploitation is the seedbed for the founding of a democratic culture.

Ellison saw little value in the attempts of black American intellectuals during the 1960s to generate critiques of the West. This is not to claim that these black writers ever succeeded in doing much more than claiming that the West was disgustingly racist, but their attempts to grasp the ways that black identity has been created and devalued by the West may be as valid and as important as any project facing the black intelligentsia today. Some of these black intellectuals recognized Ellison's Western cultural parochialism, but few could bridle their emotions sufficiently to generate a sustained rational examination. Instead of generating a comprehensive assessment of Ellison or, better yet, an analysis of the West, these black intellectuals could often muster only pathetic screams at Ellison.

It is quite likely that the repeated attacks from black nationalists and the frequent rejections from black college students during the 1960s took a toll on Ellison's psyche. Hiram Haydn, then editor of the *American Scholar*, described an incident at a 1968 editorial board meeting when Ellison vocally commandeered the entire discussion and harangued the board for over an hour and a half. Haydn claims that Ellison had no particular point to make but that his uncontrolled anger erupted after accusing the board of having disrespected him in its assigning and acceptance of articles. Concerning this event, Haydn perceptively noted,

> I suspect that this was one manifestation of the lonely burden that certain black men of a transitional generation have carried. Disclaimed by the new militants, yet too genuinely liberal for black conservatives, widely accepted by the white community, yet always aware of that *one* difference, these aristocrats of the mind and spirit have often achieved greatly in our society, yet have belonged really to no community except the small one of their peers. The strain of this isolation must eventually tell on anyone, and I believe that October evening was one time when the load was too great.[27]

After the demise of black cultural nationalism as a major force in Afro-American intellectual life, Ellison's views of Afro-American culture regained the respectability and centrality in Afro-American literary and cultural studies that they once had. Yet, as testimony to the importance of some of the black cultural nationalist claims, the resurgent Ellisonian moment in Afro-American literary and cultural studies now places varying significance on African and West Indian cultures in the development of Afro-Americans. The works of Robert Stepto, Ishmael Reed, Robert O'Meally, Lawrence Levine, Melvin Dixon, John Callahan, Kimberly Benston, Mae Henderson, Houston Baker, Stanley Crouch, Henry L. Gates, Gerald Early, Michael Harper, Darryl Dance, Horace Porter, Alan Ballard, Leon Forrest, Gary Giddens, and James Alan McPherson, among others, testify to the resurgence of an Ellisonian cultural outlook since the middle 1970s.

In one of the most publicized intellectual exchanges of the early 1960s, literary critic Irving Howe and Ralph Ellison debated the artistic role of the black writer in America and particularly the merits of the protest tradition of Afro-American fiction.[1] In the process the two men commented extensively on the sociopolitical roles of the black intellectual/writer. The ramifications of the black victim status syndrome are explicitly artistically embedded in the tradition of black protest literature. Howe and Ellison were participating in one of the central thematic debates within twentieth-century Afro-American intellectual discourse. While endorsing the victim status appeal for black writers, Howe was not acting hypocritically, for he essentially writes within a Jewish victim status syndrome. That fact has been overlooked in those commentaries of the Howe-Ellison debate intent on asserting that Howe advised black artists to act in ways different from white artists.[2] Howe's essay "Black Boys and Native Sons," originally published in *Dissent* in 1963, set the agenda for the debate.[3] After the appearance of Howe's essay Ellison was invited by the editor of the *New Leader* to respond. The essay and a rejoinder were later combined, substantially altered, and published in *Shadow and Act* under the title "The World and the Jug."[4] In my analysis of Ellison's response I use the revised essay in *Shadow and Act* as well as the original essays that appeared in the *New Leader*.

In "Black Boys and Native Sons" Howe analyzed the relationship between Richard Wright and two younger black writers, James Baldwin and Ralph Ellison, both of whom Howe considered to be Wright's protégés. Essentially, Howe is perplexed by Baldwin's, and to a lesser extent, Ellison's, decision to reject the protest tradition of Richard Wright, which, according to Howe, remained a rational and politically formidable form of black writing. Howe begins the essay by responding to Baldwin's views of the protest tradition as contained in the two Baldwin essays, "Everybody's Protest Novel" (1949) and "Many Thousands Gone" (1951).[5] In these seminal essays, Baldwin, a young and relatively unknown writer, accused the well-established Wright of creating fiction within a tradition that only allowed for the depiction of Negro characters explicitly circumscribed by societal victimization. This tradition, Baldwin argued, did not allow Wright to perceive, explore, or convey black life in all its complexity. The success of the protest novel, Baldwin argued, directly depended on the quality of the misery and despair conveyed, but the dynamics of black life, though affected by poverty and immiseration, did not respond to and depend on political-economic factors alone. Within the most wretched black poverty, universal human dynamics were constantly being acted out—struggles between mothers and daughters, fathers and sons, and sons and sons. Socioeconomic marginality had not eliminated universal human agonies from black lives.

Howe accepted Baldwin's pronouncements as the young writer's artistic intentions. In describing Baldwin's new agenda, Howe wrote, "No longer mere victim or rebel, the Negro would stand free in a self-achieved humanity."[6]

Baldwin's second essay, "Many Thousands Gone," is an elaboration on "Everybody's Protest Novel." He condemns the protest novel for its explicit embodiment of the victim status appeal insofar as it is concerned with generating a certain preordained reaction among the white readership, and in so doing, sacrifices concern for the internal dynamics of black life. Unlike "Everybody's Protest Novel," which dealt primarily with *Uncle Tom's Cabin* and, to a lesser degree, *Native Son*, "Many Thousands Gone" was aimed solely at Wright. Arguing that Bigger Thomas, the protagonist in *Native Son*, was created for no other reason but to generate guilt and fear in white America, Baldwin insisted that Wright was responsible for leading readers, especially whites, to believe that Negro life contained "no tradition, no field of manners, no possibility of ritual or intercourse, such as may, for example, sustain the Jew even after he has left his father's house."[7] Baldwin wrote of Wright's Bigger,

> For Bigger's tragedy is not that he is cold or black or hungry, not even that he is American, black; but that he has accepted a theology that denies him life, that he admits the possibility of his being sub-human and feels constrained therefore, to battle for his humanity according to those brutal criteria bequeathed him at his birth. But our humanity is our burden, our life; we need not battle for it, we need only to do what is infinitely more difficult—that is, accept it. The failure of the protest novel lies in its rejection of life, the human being, the denial of his beauty, dread, power, in its insistence that it is his categorization alone which is real and which cannot be transcended.[8]

Concerning Bigger, Baldwin later added,

> He is the monster created by the American republic, the present awful sum of generations of oppression; but to say that he is a monster is to fall into the trap of making him subhuman and he must, therefore, be made representative of a way of life which is real and human in precise ratio to the degree to which it seems to us monstrous and strange. It

seems to me that this idea carries, implicitly, a most remarkable confession: that is, that Negro life is in fact as debased and impoverished as our theology claims.

To present Bigger as a warning is simply to reinforce the American guilt and fear concerning him, it is most forcefully to limit him to that previously mentioned social arena in which he has no human validity, it is simply to condemn him to death. For he has always been a warning, he represents the evil, the sin and suffering which we are compelled to reject. . . . The courtroom, judge, jury, witnesses and spectators, recognize immediately that Bigger is their creation and they recognize this not only with hatred and fear and guilt and the resulting fury of self-righteousness but also with that morbid fullness of pride mixed with horror with which one regards the extent and power of one's wickedness. They know that death is his portion, that he runs to death; coming from darkness and dwelling in darkness, he must be, as often as he rises, banished, lest the entire planet be engulfed.[9]

Baldwin's arguments about the limitations of Wright's protest fiction are quite convincing. In forcing Bigger to scream, Wright refused to create a Bigger who also cries and whispers. However, had Bigger been portrayed otherwise, Wright might not have been able to galvanize white guilt.[10] The potential dishonesty of artistic renditions in protest fiction may be diametrically related to the genre's success as victim status propaganda.

The Baldwin attack on Richard Wright's protest literature and *Native Son* in particular has become part of Afro-American intellectual lore. The two writers met and argued at a Parisian outdoor cafe. Feeling that Baldwin, a young writer whom he had helped to win a literary scholarship, was ungrateful, Wright was angry and disappointed. Baldwin, so the story goes, at one point cried out, "The sons must slay the fathers," indicating his belief that Wright lay between himself and full artistic maturity, or even notoriety. For whatever reason, Baldwin believed that only one prominent Negro novelist could or would be allowed to surface during each generation.[11]

In contrast, Ellison claims never to have felt the need to artistically slay Wright since he would have us believe that he never viewed Wright as a literary father. Ellison has written, "No, Wright was no spiritual father of mine, certainly in no sense I recognize—nor did he pretend to be, since he felt that I had started writing too late. It was Baldwin's career not mine, that Wright proudly advanced by helping him attain the Eugene Saxton Fellowship, and it was Baldwin who found Wright a lion in his path. Being older and familiar with quite different lions in quite different paths, I simply stepped around him."[12] Howe's reading of *Native Son* differed radically from Baldwin's. He clearly appreciated Wright's intentions.

The day *Native Son* appeared, American culture was changed forever. No matter how much qualifying the book might later need, it made impossible a repetition of the old lies. In all its crudeness, melodrama, and claustrophobia of vision, Richard Wright's novel brought out into the open, as no one ever had before, the hatred, fear, and violence that have crippled and may yet destroy our culture.

A blow at the white man, the novel forced him to recognize himself as an oppressor. A blow at the black man, the novel forced him to recognize the cost of his submission. *Native Son* assaulted the most cherished of American vanities; the hope that the accumulated injustice of the past would bring with it no lasting penalties, the fantasy that in his humiliation the Negro somehow retained a sexual potency—or was it a childlike good nature:—that made it necessary to envy and still more to suppress him. . . . If such younger novelists as Baldwin and Ralph Ellison were to move beyond Wright's harsh naturalism and toward more supple modes of fiction, that was possible only because Wright had been there first, courageous enough to release the full weight of his anger.

. . . Bigger Thomas was a part of Richard Wright, a part even of the James Baldwin who stared with horror at Wright's Bigger, unable either to absorb him into his consciousness or eject him from it. Enormous courage, a discipline of self-conquest, was required to conceive Bigger Thomas, for this was no eloquent Negro spokesman, no admirable intellectual or formidable proletarian. Bigger was drawn—one would surmise, deliberately—from white fantasy and white contempt. Bigger was the worst of Negro life accepted, then rendered a trifle conscious and thrown back at those who had made him what he was.

"No American Negro exists," Baldwin would later write, "who does not have his private Bigger Thomas living in the skull."[13]

Contrary to superficial interpretations of Howe's arguments, such as Robert Penn Warren's in *Who Speaks for the Negro*, "Black Boys and Native Sons" is quite engaging. Howe expressed deep admiration for Wright's boldness, particularly his willingness to confront the "worst of Negro life." He credited Wright for stepping outside of the "we can be respectable too" theme and the "aren't they cute" humor that had dominated black literature for generations.[14]

In praising Wright's bravery, Howe did not excuse his artistic shortcomings as some of his critics, including Ellison, have falsely accused. Though Howe praised *Invisible Man* in the essay, he expressed discomfort at what he took to be the overarching ideological ethos of Ellison. Howe quoted from Ellison's discussion of his artistic intent in *Invisible Man*. "Thus to see America with an awareness of its rich diversity and its almost magical fluidity and freedom, I was forced to conceive of a novel unburdened by the narrow naturalism which has led after so many triumphs to the final and unrelieved despair which marks so much of our current fiction."[15] In response to Ellison, Howe wrote, "This note of willed affirmation—as if one could *decide* one's deepest and most authentic response to society!—was to be heard in many of the works of the fifties."[16] Elaborating further on Ellison's rather doctrinaire bourgeois conception of freedom in *Invisible Man*, Howe stated,

> Still more troublesome, both as it breaks the coherence of the novel and reveals Ellison's dependence on the post-war Zeitgeist, is the sudden, unprepared, and implausible assertion of unconditioned freedom with which the novel ends. . . .
>
> . . . Nor is one easily persuaded by the hero's discovery that "my world had become one of infinite possibilities," his refusal to be the "invisible man" whose body is manipulated by various social groups. Though the unqualified assertion of self-liberation was a favorite strategy among American literary people in the fifties, it is also vapid and insubstantial. It violates the reality of social life, the interplay between external conditions and personal will, quite as much as the determinism of the thirties. The unfortunate fact remains that to de-

fine one's individuality is to stumble upon social barriers which stand in the way, all too much in the way, of "infinite possibilities." Freedom can be fought for, but it cannot always be willed or asserted into existence. And it seems hardly an accident that even as Ellison's hero asserts the "infinite possibilities" he makes no attempt to specify them.[17]

Howe's critique of the limitations of Ellison's notion of freedom is quite devastating. In many respects his analysis echoes the Merleau-Ponty discussion of the conception of freedom found in Sartre's *Being and Nothingness*. Howe recognized the romantic conception of the heroic that runs throughout Ellison's novel. Because Ellison's depictions of freedom and heroic possibility were romantic, they were ahistorical and acontextual in character. As such, Ellison's formulations would always be vulnerable to discussions that placed the individual will in a more dialectical relationship with the external world. Ellison, who prided himself on transcending the crude limits of strict social determinism, must have been angered by Howe's insistence that his conception was equally simplistic and one-sided.

Yet, I suspect that what bothered Ellison most about Howe's statements was not the critique of his notion of freedom but Howe's insinuations that in writing in a nonprotest manner, Ellison had been less ethnically responsible than Wright. Howe had written,

> For Wright was perhaps justified in not paying attention to the changes that have occurred in the South these past decades. When Negro liberals write that despite the prevalence of bias there has been an improvement in the life of their people, such statements are reasonable and necessary. But what have these to do with the way Negroes feel, with the power of memories they must surely retain? About this we know very little and would be well advised not to nourish preconceptions, for their feelings may be much closer to Wright's rasping outbursts than to the more modulated tones of some younger Negro novelists. Wright remembered, and what he remembered other Negroes must also have remembered. And in that way he kept faith with the experience of the boy who had bought his way out of the depths, to speak for those who remained there.[18]

He would later rhetorically ask Ellison, "In what ways can a Negro writer—indeed any Negro—achieve 'personal realization' as long as the American Negro remain oppressed? To what extent can he achieve 'personal realization' apart from the common effort of his people to win their full freedom? To what extent can he present a valid portrait of American Negro life without bringing in 'plight and protest?' "[19]

Ellison replied,

I do not understand why Howe thinks I said anything on the subject of writing about "Negro experience" in a manner which excludes what he calls "plight and protest"; he must have gotten his Negroes mixed. But as to answering his question concerning the "ways a Negro writer can achieve personal realization apart from the common effort of his people to win their full freedom", I suggest that he ask himself in what way shall a Negro writer achieve personal realization (as writer) *after* his people have won their full freedom? The answer appears to be the same in both instances: He will have to go it alone! He must suffer alone even as he shares the suffering of his group, and he must write alone and pit his talents against the standards set by the best practitioners of the craft, both past and present in any case. For the writer's real way of sharing the experience of his group is to convert its mutual suffering into lasting value. Is Howe suggesting, incidentally, that Heinrich Heine did not exist?[20]

Howe's statement and Ellison's reply are somewhat disingenuous. Howe had asked if a Negro writer, or any Negro, could achieve personal realization if black Americans as a group remain oppressed. Despite the nebulous meaning of "personal realization," the question raised the generic issue of a black individual's collective ethnic identity. In writing as if a black individual had to wait until all blacks were free (whatever that is), Howe appears to be denying the possibility for contemporary black individuality. Worse, the overstatement implies that no black American has ever achieved personal realization, given the continuing history of Afro-American oppression.

Ellison, ever the individualist, sidesteps the crux of Howe's question to assert that the individual writer achieves personal realization as a writer *only* through his or her individual mastery of written forms. Yet Ellison also claims that the individual writer "shares the suffering of his group."[21] This paradoxical response is resolved through Ellison's dialectical belief that through writing, the writer can simultaneously express a collective consciousness with his or her ethnic peers and personally realize his or her individuality as only individual artists can. In Ellison's logic the writer appears to have no other way of identifying with his or her ethnic group (or community at large) except through his or her writing. It is as if the writer is a completely one-dimensional creature, a disembodied writing machine void of the multitude of linkages to self and others that most of us experience.

Howe, in overemphasizing collective identities, and Ellison, in overstating individual ones, were simultaneously unable to confront the complexity of the individual writer's relationship to his or her oppressed ethnic group. Howe viewed Ellison's claims for individuality as a privilege of the non-oppressed. Ellison, in invoking Heine, questioned the validity of Howe's formulations for Howe and other Jewish intellectuals. Did Howe, Trilling, and Bellow assess the validity of their own individual artistic achievements via reference to the quality of freedom experienced by all Jews? If not, why did Howe grant individual Jewish writers freedoms that he did not grant to individual black American artists?

Ellison did not view himself as having broken faith with his black ancestors. Crucial to Ellison's aesthetic formulations was his effort to posit himself as an elaborator of the folk culture of the black masses and thus explicitly in touch with the collective memory of his ethnic group. This is in part why Ellison did not respond to Howe by merely proclaiming his right as an artist to write about anything he so desired as long as he did so with skill and honesty. Mistakenly, commentators have often assumed that Ellison's response to Howe in "The World and the Jug" is an argument in behalf of black artistic/intellectual freedom. In fact, Ellison implicitly accepts Howe's claim that a black novelist should articulate the views and struggles of the black masses, but he disagrees over the substance of those views and struggles and how they should be conveyed artistically. Ellison is therefore caught having to justify to Howe his particular approach to writing on the grounds that it accurately portrays black life. This is after all why Ellison spends so much time in his response depicting a material reality of black life that differs from Howe's perceptions. It is as if Ellison wanted to present a realist defense of his antirealistic approach to art.

Considering the lavish praise bestowed on Wright by Howe, it should not have been surprising that Howe advised Baldwin and Ellison to follow in Wright's footsteps. Howe advises them to maintain the umbilical cord of the victim status. He tells them to continue to shock "us"— white Americans—with the rage that we know must be in you as a result of the way that we have treated you. Do not spare us the pain and the anger. Howe raised a question—"How could a Negro put pen to paper, how could he so much as think or breathe without some impulsion to protest, be it harsh or mild, political or private, released or buried? The 'sociology' of his existence formed a constant pressure on his literary work and not merely in the way this might be true for any writer, but with a pain and ferocity that nothing could remove."[22]

Howe's rhetorical question exposes a sentiment that is almost stereotypically "old" American Left. Besides a residue of racial paternalism, it reflects the tendency of American leftist intellectuals who came of age during the 1930s and 1940s to appropriate an "economistic" analytical framework that rendered individuals as respondents "in the final analysis" to their socioeconomic situation.[23] This view has remained with his generation of American leftist thinkers ever since, despite the infiltration of Freudian thought, the rejection of Communism, and the challenges of Critical Theory and Gramscian ideas. Those most oppressed in society, according to this logic, would be the most enraged sector of the society, and justifiably so. Black Americans were often thought to be latent revolutionaries in waiting, seething with a deep anger, ready to explode should something out of the ordinary trigger that which was repressed.[24] Like Richard Wright, who repeatedly articulated economic Marxist assumptions in his early fiction, Howe too was economistic. Yet Howe was not an economic determinist to the extent that Ellison would attribute to him. Was Howe's view so absurd? As a believer in the pervasive power of social conditionality, Howe was led to assume that Afro-Americans, that is, rational Afro-Americans who cared about the plight of their ethnic group, would harbor deep anger and resentment toward the United States that would be articulated in protest. Had not James Baldwin admitted that there is a bit of Bigger Thomas in every Negro?

Ellison has maintained that a socially determined Bigger Thomas was not a fact of Negro life but an image created by the black and liberal white social-scientific imagination. Wright had supposedly appropriated this image through either the social-scientific Marx or his affiliation with the Chicago school of sociology. To Ellison, any theory or argument that purports to have discovered unique boundaries and finite consistencies to the ways that blacks think, feel, or act is too restrictive to capture Negro humanity.[25] The material world, according to Ellison, has a drastically limited impact on the lives of people. It is merely the setting upon which people act. Howe's social determinism, as well as his views concerning the suffering and anger of the Negro that led him to advocate a quasi-straitjacket of protest for the Negro writer, were Marxian influenced. Ellison, in challenging Howe on this point, wanted to challenge all social deterministic theories, not simply Marxism. Instead of simply asserting that all Negroes were not singularly concerned about political freedom and that he was one such Negro, Ellison is forced to make exaggerated claims about the autonomy of individuals from socioeconomic factors when in fact Ellison's own cultural theory rests upon notions of cultural determinism. Ellison attempts to deny any and all possible structural (read material) causes for consistencies in Afro-American culture over time, but is culture dropped like manna from heaven? If culture ultimately involves ways that people humanize their environment, it seems plausible that changes in social environments lead to changes in culture over time. Though perhaps rhetorically and literarily expedient, Ellison's belief in the potential transcendence of the will over all obstacles is quite specious. The will and the psyche are ensconced in culture. What, one might ask, could be more coercive of individuality than culture?[26]

Whether or not one agrees with Ellison's belief that social deterministic theories deny humanity, it is apparent that social deterministic theories often encompass what sociologist Dennis Wrong referred to as an "over socialized conception of man."[27] Political programs premised on an overbearing social determinism have often failed in black America for reasons that Ellison in part, articulates. Black people are more than victims. Regardless of the degree of oppression, blacks do not live by power or powerlessness alone. For instance, Communism as a political movement and ideology for rendering the world rational was never accepted as valid by most of the black Americans who were exposed to it during its American heyday in the 1930s, for reasons that may in part be perceived from Ellison's argument.[28] Why, one might ask, was the Commu-

nist Party un ... ‹merica
as it did in wl ... in light
of the dire p ... ‹ might
argue that be ... ‹istic in
the shifts the ... e determined by So ... nerica),
they were ign ... ommu-
nists were inf ... ‹italism
imprisoned t ... people
may have bee ... ‹d time
trying to teac ... Ameri-
can dream. I ... ‹ve and
hate, to perf... josn Gibson's batting stance, to jab like joe Louis, to dance like "Snake Hips," or to write like Ernest Hemingway to be imbued with unrelenting desires for social protest. The idea that oppressed peoples would be engaged in activities other than those solely intent on political emancipation has always been baffling to economistic Leftists like Howe and Wright. In the eyes of such thinkers, the non-economic concerns of the poor appear frivolous. Why would a Negro man be concerned about whether or not his suit was pressed properly when he could not attend decent schools? Because, as Ellison knows, he just might have a date that evening with a woman he desires. It is these occurrences, the tribulations and torments of self-creation in everyday life, that Ellison highlights for a Howe who may not have appreciated how little time many blacks spent pondering their oppression.

For the economistic Howe, however, the authentic voice of the oppressed black community, the voice not tinged with false consciousness, is the voice of outrage. Though Howe may not have been aware of the attitudes toward black life that Ellison discussed, he knew all too well that Ellison was in part romanticizing a bleak situation. Who could deny, for instance, that Josh Gibson's life was not peculiarly damaged in a way that Gibson was conscious of because he could not use the baseball talents he worked so hard to develop to attain the status that he knew he deserved? Who could deny that the promise that America held out to whites, an awareness that Ellison often mentions, would not embitter and warp blacks who endured years of frustration and hypocrisy? In effect, by claiming that politics was merely one facet of black existence and perhaps not its most important component, Ellison is trapped into denying just how deeply the white treatment of blacks affected black life materially and psychologically.

Ellison informs Howe that his statements concerning the "pain and ferocity" of the Negro situation that "nothing could remove" remind him of what someone had said to him just prior to the publication of *Invisible Man*: that he had suffered too much as a Negro to allow him to "achieve that psychological and emotional distance necessary for artistic creation."[30] Ellison stated:

> Evidently Howe feels that unrelieved suffering is the only "real" Negro experience, and that the true Negro writer must be ferocious.
>
> But there is also an American Negro tradition which teaches one to deflect racial provocation and to master and contain pain. It is a tradition which abhors as obscene any trading on one's own anguish for gain or sympathy; which springs not from a desire to deny the harshness of existence but from a will to deal with it as men at their best have always done. It takes fortitude to be a man and no less to be an artist. Perhaps it takes even more if the black man would be an artist. If so, there are no exemptions. It would seem to me, therefore, that the question of how the "sociology of his existence" presses upon a Negro writer's work depends upon how much of his life the individual writer is able to transform into art. What moves a writer to eloquence is less meaningful than what he makes of it. How much, by the way, do we know of Sophocles' wounds?
>
> One unfamiliar with what Howe stands for would get the impression that when he looks at a Negro he sees not a human being but an abstract embodiment of living hell.[31]

Ellison loathes Howe's attempt to lecture him on the proper way of being an authentic black writer and black person. Though Ellison claims otherwise, he is clearly annoyed by a white critic who, though divorced from the responsibilities, burdens, and joys of black life, is willing to provide unsolicited advice to black authors on how to remain true to their blackness. Ellison began his response to Howe in the following manner:

First, three questions: Why is it so often true that when critics confront the American as *Negro* they suddenly drop their advanced critical armament and revert with an air of confident superiority to quite primitive modes of analysis? Why is it that sociology-oriented critics seem to rate literature so far below politics and ideology that they would rather kill a novel than modify their presumptions concerning a given reality which it seeks in its own terms to project? Finally, why is it that so many of those who would tell us the meaning of Negro life never bother to learn how varied it really is?[32]

Ellison would certainly be correct in rejecting Howe's or anyone's pretentions of being able to judge the greatness of Negro literature by standards other than and inferior to those used to judge the greatness of other literatures. Such judgments are predicated upon the assumption that Negro writers are not in the same literary league as their white peers. In this sense, Ellison realized that the Jewish Howe, however unwillingly, speaks with the voice of the authoritative white critic with all of the power invested in him by mainstream intellectual discourse (read white intellectual discourse) to pronounce upon the work of cultural upstarts. Ellison, on the other hand, does not shy away from clothing himself in blackness, a tactic that allows him to affect the air of the knowledgeable native against the aggressive, ignorant interloper/colonizer. Howe recognizes that Ellison uses his insider status as a way of proclaiming privileged knowledge about the Negro and subsequently does not dare confront Ellison on any of the specific statements that Ellison makes about Negroes, some of which are highly debatable.[33]

There is little in Howe's essay that could be used to substantiate Ellison's claims about Howe, for Howe not only judges Wright artistically but finds him wanting.[34] Ellison misses Howe's point. Wright is, according to Howe, an important intellectual figure despite being a lesser artist. Ellison argues that the only valid criteria to use to assess Wright are formal literary criteria. Howe attempts to grasp the significance of Wright as a black intellectual on the American intellectual scene and within the broader society. Howe believes that the significance of any novel has much to do with the cultural context in which it is both written and received. Ellison believes that these issues are but sideshows. The real issue is the artistic merits of the work. As such, he is concerned that Wright was not a great artist.

From Howe's vantage point the publication of Wright's *Native Son* is a far more significant event intellectually than the publication of Ellison's *Invisible Man*. In his ahistorical and acontextual understanding of literature Ellison refuses to judge any work of art by criteria other than its artistic merits. Yet Ellison is correct when he claims that Howe did not judge Wright's work solely as a work of art.[35] Ellison stated:

> I knew even then, that protest is not the source of the inadequacy characteristic of most novels by Negroes, but the simple failure of craft, bad writing; the desire to have protest perform the difficult tasks of art; the belief that racial suffering, social injustice or ideologies of whatever mammy-made variety, is enough. . . .
>
> I agree with Howe that protest is an element of all art, though it does not necessarily take the form of speaking for a political or social program. It might appear in a novel as a technical assault against the styles which have gone before, or as protest against the human condition. If *Invisible Man* is even "apparently" free from "the ideological and emotional penalties suffered by Negroes in this country," it is because I tried to the best of my ability to transform these elements into art. My goal was not to escape, or hold back, but to work through to transcend, as the blues transcend the painful conditions with which they deal. The protest is there, not because I was helpless before my racial condition, but because I put it there. If there is anything "miraculous" about the book it is the result of hard work undertaken in the belief that the work of art is important in itself, that it is a social action in itself.[36]

In the exchange with Howe, one senses that Ellison is correct in proclaiming a wider diversity and deeper complexity to black life than Howe may have been willing to admit or able to perceive. Yet, there was truth in Howe's claim that the oppression of blacks must have stifled a great deal of the creative powers and expression of black people. The diversity of black life, though broad, is not as unlimited as Ellison would have us think. Furthermore, given his insistence on the diversity of black life, how is it that Ellison denies the existence of a Bigger Thomas? Ellison appears to deny the possibility of Bigger Thomas precisely because he denies the possibility of Negroes who have been utterly warped by racial and class oppression.

Ellison was not always silent on the devastating impact of black oppression on black American lives. In "Harlem Is Nowhere," an essay written in 1948, he described a Harlem that both nurtured and severely stifled black life:

> Hence the most surreal fantasies are acted out upon the streets of Harlem; a man ducks in and out of traffic shouting and throwing imaginary grenades that actually exploded during World War I; a boy participates in the rape-robbery of his mother; a man beating his wife in a park uses boxing "science" and observes Marquess of Queensberry rules (no rabbit punching, no blows beneath the belt); two men hold a third while a lesbian slashes him to death with a razor blade; boy gangsters wielding homemade pistols . . . shoot down their rivals.[37]

The young Ellison recognized a degree of social anomie among blacks in Harlem. Sounding like a Chicago school sociologist, Ellison wrote,

> When Negroes are barred from participating in the main institutional life of society they lose far more than economic privileges or the satisfaction of saluting the flag with unmixed emotions. They lose one of the bulwarks which men place between themselves and the constant threat of chaos. For whatever the assigned function of social institutions, their psychological function is to protect the citizen against the irrational, incalculable forces that hover about the edges of human life like cosmic destruction lurking within an atomic stockpile.
>
> And it is precisely the denial of this support through segregation and discrimination that leaves the most balanced Negro open to anxiety.[38]

By the mid-1960s, Ellison had discarded such materialist arguments as those in "Harlem Is Nowhere." Instead, Ellison assumed a view of human life that posited all cultures as equally rich, including that of the Harlem Negro. Not only did he adhere to this as an anthropological assumption, but he also appeared to treat it as an empirical fact. In response to Howe's assertions that American racism had devastated black life, Ellison wrote,

> He [Howe] seems never to have considered that American Negro life (and here he is encouraged by certain Negro "spokesmen") is, for the Negro who must live it, not only a burden (and not always that) but also a discipline—just as any human life which has endured so long is a discipline teaching its own insights into the human condition, its own strategies of survival. There is a fullness, even a richness here; and here despite the realities of politics, perhaps, but nevertheless here and real. Because it is human life. And Wright, for all of his indictments, was no less its product than that other talented Mississippian, Leontyne Price. To deny in the interest of revolutionary posture that such possibilities of human richness exist for others, even in Mississippi, is not only to deny us our humanity but to betray the critic's commitment to social reality. Critics who do so should abandon literature for politics.[39]

Ellison disagrees with those arguments which claim that black life in Jim Crow Mississippi was definitively repressed and stifled. Moreover, he interprets such arguments as denials of the humanity of black Mississippians. Ellison has woven an intellectual defense of black equality that appears to render any recognition of the detrimental impact of racism on black lives potentially threatening to the validation of Negro humanity.

The problem for Ellison lies in his appropriation of the blues as a philosophy of life. If, as Ellison argues, the attraction of the blues lies in their expression of agony and the possibility of conquering agony through sheer toughness of spirit, what room is there for utter human defeat? If the blues provide no solution and offer no scapegoat but the self, who is to blame for the destruction of Negroes but Negroes themselves? Blacks destroyed by racism are testimonies of the weakness of the black will, and ultimately of black people. If, as Ellison assumed, blacks were not destroyed by slavery, it is difficult for him to imagine black destruction at the hands of less brutal, more contemporary oppression. Yet, such destruction occurs now as it did during slavery, and it is not self-destruction. Ellison's claim that slaves, instead of freedom, had songs, dance, and folklore is as disingenuous as his more contemporary claim that modern black life and culture condition blacks to deal with their plight.[40] Ellison has argued,

> For even as his life toughens the Negro, even as it brutalizes him, sensitizes him, dulls him, goads him to anger, moves him to irony, sometimes fracturing and sometimes affirming his hopes; even as it shapes his attitudes toward family, sex, love, religion; even as it modulates his humor, tempers his joy—it conditions him to deal with his life and with himself. Because it is his life and no mere abstraction in someone's head. He must live it and try consciously to grasp its complexity until he can change it; must live it as he changes it. He is no mere product of his socio-political predicament. He is a product of the interaction between his racial predicament, his individual will and the broader American cultural freedom in which he finds his ambiguous existence. Thus he, too, in a limited way, is his own creation.[41]

Insofar as the blues philosophy of life is but one culturally specific manifestation of universal human dilemmas, the blues philosophy links black culture to humanity in general. Ellison places the blues within a neosocial-scientific, functionalist framework. This framework and its implied cultural relativism allow Ellison to posit cultural equality for all peoples. Yet, like any functionalist, Ellison asserts the existence of certain universal needs, habits, and human dilemmas and assumes that these needs must be met, habits practiced, and dilemmas confronted if people, any people, are to endure.[42] As a result, functionalism often determines what the investigator will find before he or she investigates. For Ellison, functionalism allows him to argue that the complexity of human life is the same for the slave and the slave master. They each experience love, hatred, irony, and sadness. This complexity exists for all peoples regardless of their socioeconomic and political contexts.

Insofar as Wright created in Bigger Thomas a character almost completely determined by his environment, Ellison argues that Bigger Thomas is a distortion of black life. Authentic blacks would have developed cultural strategies for psychologically coping with the material impoverishment that trapped Bigger Thomas. They would have displayed some type of human agency. Whether through the church, sports, music, or urban folklore, the majority of direly impoverished black slum-dwelling Chicagoans in the 1940s found some way to sustain meaning in their lives. After all, most black Chicagoans did not rape, murder, and throw women off tenement roofs. Instead, Wright created a Bigger who was crushed by his environment.

Hidden behind Ellison's desire to proclaim potential human mastery over any social situation is also the claim that social situations are seldom as desperate as social scientists depict them. In hopes of portraying the richness, depth, and diversity of black life, Ellison tinkers with rendering epiphenomenal much of the oppression of blacks. His views of blacks do not include room for any "marks of oppression." Ellison has argued that Wright could imagine a Bigger Thomas but Bigger could not have imagined Richard Wright. He is correct in insisting that Wright did not create in *Native Son* a depiction of Chicago that allowed for the rise of other would-be Richard Wrights. Ellison could not admit then and may not be able to admit now that there are thousands if not tens of thousands of blacks like Bigger Thomas who could not and cannot imagine a Richard Wright.

Quite unlike the post–*Invisible Man* Ellison, Wright always believed that racism and class oppression took a dire toll on black life. In *Black Boy*, Wright had written,

(After I had outlived the shocks of childhood, after the habit of reflection had been born in me, I used to mull over the strange absence of real kindness in Negroes, how unstable was our tenderness, how lacking in genuine passion we were, how void of great hope, how timid our joy, how bare our traditions, how hollow our memories, how lacking we were in those intangible sentiments that bind man to man and how shallow was even our despair. After I had learned other ways of life I used to brood upon the unconscious irony of those who felt that Negroes led so passionate an existence! I saw that what had been taken for our emotional strength was our negative confusions, our flights, our fears, our frenzy under pressure.

(Whenever I thought of the essential bleakness of black life in America, I knew that Negroes had never been allowed to catch the full spirit of Western civilization, that they lived somehow in it but not of it. And when I brooded upon the cultural barrenness of black life, I wondered if clean, positive tenderness, love, honor, loyalty and the capacity to remember were native with man. I asked myself if these human qualities were not fostered, won, struggled and suffered for, preserved in ritual from one generation to another.)[43]

In raising such questions, Wright violated Ellison's victim status ideology, for Ellison essentially perceived Wright's questions as assaults on the humanity of black people.[44] Ellison stated, "For me keeping faith would never allow me to even raise such a question about any segment of humanity."[45] Why was Wright so willing and able to violate Ellisonian sacred cows? Ellison finds the answer in Wright's Marxism: "How awful that Wright found the facile answers of Marxism before he learned to use literature as a means for discovering the forms of American Negro humanity. I could not and cannot question their existence, I can only seek again and again to project that humanity as I see it and feel it."[46]

The claim that the facile answers of Marxism blinded Wright to black humanity is either a statement of willed ignorance or a polemical falsehood. As a former leftist, Ellison knew that within the facility of Marxism there existed no such creature as an individual void of humanity. For Richard Wright the humanity of blacks was never in question. Ellison's argument may have been on firmer ground had he claimed that Wright denied the humanity of blacks *despite* his Marxism. In appropriating Marxism, Wright found a social philosophy that affirmed the humanity of oppressed blacks. Not only did Ellison know this, but he had previously acknowledged it in his 1945 essay, "Richard Wright's Blues."[47] Unlike the author of *Native Son*, the mature Ellison had an understanding of humanity that was undoubtedly similar to Malraux's. In *The Voices of Silence*, Malraux stated that "humanism does not consist in saying: 'No animal could have done what we have done,' but in declaring: 'We have refused to do what the beast within us willed to do.'"[48] For Ellison, Bigger Thomas had yielded to the beast within.

Ellison should have admitted that he and Wright simply disagreed over the degree to which human beings were determined by their environment.[49] He may have disagreed with the way that individuality was defined by Wright, but Ellison cannot honestly claim, given Wright's view of humanity, that Wright created inhuman blacks. In Wright's view, individuals are inherently social creatures.[50] They are human by the fact of their existence. Their humanity is not predicated upon the creation of cultural artifacts such as the blues. An individual who is as oppressed, repressed, and distorted as Bigger Thomas is not void of humanity but is forced to live a wretched and alienated existence. He had not been allowed to fulfill his human destiny.

Ellison's claim that Wright's ideology led him to write protest novels is undoubtedly correct. Furthermore, protest fiction did not allow Wright the artistic space to write of "a Negro as intelligent, as creative or as dedicated as himself."[51] But it is also true that Ellison's ideology did not allow him to write protest novels or to write about a Bigger Thomas. Both writers conveyed limited perspectives of black life.[52] Ellison's writings appear more encompassing of black life to many contemporary intellectuals and literary critics. I suggest that the attraction to Ellison's views of black life at the expense of Wright's stems from three major sources: (1) Ellison's artistic superiority over Wright, (2) the ethnically therapeutic uses of an Ellisonian view of black life in an era of ethnic affirmation, and (3) the mere fact that most literary critics and scholars have not lived in conscious contact with figures like Bigger Thomas and thus are ignorant of Bigger's absence in Ellison's work.[53]

Ellison's blues ontology generates a less critical framework than Wright's Marxism for confronting the political situation of blacks precisely because Ellison viewed the political-social order as a relatively insignificant shaper of black life. Why protest against a society that lacks the power to devastate black life? Ellison perceived the distorting ramifications of a history of racial and economic oppression on black life as far less intense and profound than those perceived by Wright. The differences in their perceptions of racism's impact on black Americans are quite phenomenal.

Consequently, much, though not all, of what Ellison considers to have been the influence of Wright's adherence to a social protest ideology in his writing is in fact a result of Wright's differing perception of the plight of black Americans. Wright did not write protest fiction merely because he had "found the facile answers of Marxism before he learned to use literature as a means for discovering the forms of American Negro humanity." He wrote protest fiction because he saw more to protest about in America than Ellison did.[54] Ellison would have us believe that he and Wright shared a similar social vision but that unlike Wright, who expressed anger in unbridled rage, he was able to bridle his rage and create true art. On one occasion in 1955, Ellison frankly admitted, "Most of the social realists of the period were concerned less with tragedy than injustice. *I wasn't and am not, primarily concerned with injustice but with art.*"55

It should not be surprising that Wright, who lived an extremity that Ellison had not, would be more angry at America than was Ellison. Wright's life in the South and later in Chicago exposed him to American racial and class oppression in a way that Ellison never experienced and does not and perhaps cannot admit to being ignorant of. Ellison writes, as if he had experienced Wright's life and more (as if life experiences could be compared on a linear scale), "I had been a Negro for twenty-two or twenty-three years when I met Wright and in more places and under a greater variety of circumstances than he had then known."56

Ellison's views of the Jim Crow South reflected his perceptions of the less than drastic plight of black life there. His views actually border on a romanticization of southern black life. Ellison's response to what he considered Howe's simplification of black life is a case in point. Howe's "simplification" was the claim that black life had been distorted by southern racist oppression. Ellison's response, though personal, is meant to convey a universality. "For oddly enough, I found it far less painful to have to move to the back of a Southern bus, or climb to the peanut gallery of a movie house—matters about which I could do nothing except walk, read, hunt, dance, sculpt, cultivate ideas, or seek other uses for my time—than to tolerate concepts which distorted the actual reality of my situation or my reactions to it."57

When reading Ellison's perceptions of the South one must remember that he did not experience the South from the vantage point of a native black southerner. Ellison's sense of possibility was decidedly that of a black raised outside the Deep South. At no time did he have any reason to doubt that his stay in Alabama would be temporary. Qualitatively, Ellison only experienced the periphery of southern black life during the age of Jim Crow. Who but Ellison would have argued that attendance at a southern black college, life in a college town, and journeys to the countryside with the Tuskegee band would substantively immerse him in black life in the Deep South? Is it not at all surprising that Ellison could proclaim that his sense of self was not determined by southern laws and mores? We should not view this psychological autonomy as in any way typical of black southerners. As many sociological studies of the South during that time have shown, there was a tremendous psychological price paid by southern black people for their years of constant repression. One need only read Hortense Powdermaker's *After Freedom* (1939); Allison Davis, Burleigh Gardner, and Mary Gardner's *Deep South* (1941); or Allison Davis and John Dollard's *Children of Bondage* (1937) to document this point.[58] Ellison conspicuously overlooks the fact that segregation was the institutionalized reinforcement of a powerful antiblack stigma as well as a legitimator of racially determined unequal material existences. In his passion to hide what is essentially a "sour grapes" attitude toward that which was denied to him and other blacks for racist reasons, Ellison never explicitly confronts the fact that separate was unequal. While writing extensively about the mistaken assumption among white southerners that Negroes craved to live physically integrated with them, Ellison appears to be responding to the argument that separate was inherently unequal. In arguing that blacks no more wanted to be "white" than whites wanted to be "black," Ellison overlooks the fact that black southerners wanted many of the things associated with being white and if given the chance would have, in many instances, relinquished the "wholeness" of black life to pursue them. Needless to say, some blacks did want to be white.

An example of Ellison's sour grapes attitude was revealed in his response to Howe's claims concerning the impact of racism on Ellison's life. According to Howe, "the young Ralph Ellison, even while reading these great writers, could not in Macon County attend the white man's school or movie house."[59] Ellison sidesteps Howe's point. He claims that he never wanted to be able to attend a white school anyway since the famous composer that he desired to study with taught at Tuskegee. This composer, Ellison claimed, was probably the best classical musician in the Southeast. Never once in his reply does Ellison confront Howe's point that whether or not he had desired to attend Tuskegee Institute, it was one of the few colleges that he could have attended in the 1930s. It was as if Ellison could not admit to Howe that racial segregation had significantly constrained his life's choices. More significantly, he could not confront the possibility that Tuskegee was intellectually inferior to Howe's City College of New York. Howe and Ellison both knew that Tuskegee had never been an intellectual bastion. Yet, Ellison could not admit the inferiority of black institutions for reasons that apparently have to do with his feelings that any admission that he was denied equality by being refused access to white institutions was somehow an attack on black institutions and thus black people. He equated it with an admission of black inferiority precisely because the logic of his notion of humanity did not allow him to explain the inferiority of these institutions by a social conditionality thesis. Yet on another occasion when he was not addressing "the white intellectual," Ellison spoke more honestly about Tuskegee. Before an audience at the Bank Street College of Education, Ellison said,

> Much of the education that I received at Tuskegee (now this isn't quite true of Oklahoma City) was an education away from the uses of the imagination, away from the attitudes of aggression and courage.
>
> . . . One of the worst things for a teacher to do to a Negro child is to treat him as though he were completely emasculated of potentiality. And this, I'm sorry to say, is what I have found Negro teachers doing. Not all, fortunately, but far too many. At Tuskegee during the '30's most of the teachers would not speak to a student outside the classroom. The students resented it, I resented it—I'll speak personally—I could never take them very seriously as teachers. Something was in the way. A fatal noise had been introduced into the communication.[60]

This Bank Street lecture was delivered in September 1963, several months prior to Ellison's response to Howe.

Horace Cayton, the black sociologist who had trained at the University of Chicago, was a visiting professor at Tuskegee during the late 1930s. He reflected on his stay there in his autobiography, *Long Old Road*.

> The first group I came into intimate contact with were my fellow faculty members in the residence hall. Most were southern Negroes, some of whom had attended northern universities. For the most part they had only B.A. degrees and were working towards their master's. On the whole their intellectual level seemed to me low, although for the most part they were teaching students from plantations who were not themselves adequately prepared even for high school work. My graduate work at the University of Chicago left me little in common with these ill-prepared teachers, who were not even very interested in their work, and more disturbing was their attitude toward their stu-

dents. There was a strict caste line between students and faculty; the faculty looked down on the students as ignorant sharecroppers.

But I soon discovered that if the teachers held the students in contempt, most students were equally scornful of the faculty. A majority of them were well past high school age, and they were linked together against not only the faculty but also the rigid, puritanical college rules. The student attitude I found not dissimilar to the resistance many southern Negroes employed against whites.[61]

Even though Cayton apparently exhibited an extraordinary condescension toward black southerners and the less well educated, his views of Tuskegee's intellectual climate cannot be dismissed.

At times Ellison's defense of the significant presence of black freedom lurking within the Deep South during the 1930s reached fantastic proportions. Howe referred to Ellison as "out of control" when Ellison attempted to argue that Howe's alleged distortions of black life were far more fearful to him than the actual treatment of blacks in Mississippi. Ellison had stated,

I fear the implications of Howe's ideas concerning the Negro writer's role as actionist more than I do the State of Mississippi. Which is not to deny the viciousness which exists there but to recognize the degree of freedom which also exists there precisely because the repression is relatively crude, or at least it was during Wright's time, and it left the world of literature alone. William Faulkner lived neither in Jefferson nor Frenchman's Bend but in Oxford. He, too, was a Mississippian, just as the boys who helped Wright leave Jackson were the sons of a Negro college president. Both Faulkner and these boys must be recognized as part of the social reality of Mississippi.[62]

Ellison's invocation of the exceptional individual as the standard-bearer for masses of people was not racially restricted. Heroes could be found anywhere. The logic of his argument could lead to the conclusion that the repression of the arts under Stalin was not as dire as we had once thought, since Aleksandr Solzhenitsyn continued to write. The use of the exceptional as the standard-bearer for "a people" is typical of Ellison. He appears to ignore the obvious fact that the contours of the normal existence for blacks in Mississippi were not conducive to the production of Leontyne Prices. Furthermore, there was but one William Faulkner in Oxford. Ellison, in viewing Wright and Faulkner as the standard-bearers for their respective southern communities, denied the agony, fear, and frustration of many of those Mississippians who did not have the opportunity to become Wrights or Faulkners.

Though Ellison had admitted at Bank Street that Tuskegee was not an especially intellectual environment, he had found a few exceptional teachers there who were committed and able. William Dawson and Hazel Harrison were such persons.[63] Another was Morteza Sprague, the literature instructor to whom Ellison dedicated *Shadow and Act*.[64] It is an exceptional person like Sprague who in Ellison's eyes embodies the group's potential. In fact, the ability to realize human potential in the face of various impediments designates a person as exceptional. Concerning the exceptional Richard Wright, Ellison wrote, "No matter how strictly Negroes are segregated socially and politically, on the level of the imagination their ability to achieve freedom is limited only by their individual aspiration, insight, energy and will. Wright was able to free himself in Mississippi because he had the imagination and the will to do so."[65] It is doubtful that Wright ever considered himself free in Mississippi simply because he could imagine life under other circumstances. Ellison's notion of freedom is void of materiality and is one that the Marxist-influenced Wright would have thought absurd.[66] Howe certainly thought it was. It is an idea of freedom that is too divorced from behavior even to be considered liberal. Conspicuously absent from Ellison's notion of freedom is any mention of opportunity. Ellison does not believe that freedom can be denied by external forces. Freedom is ultimately in the mind, a function of the will and the imagination. Alas, according to Ellison, the writer experiences freedom in writing. Yet Howe recognized that even the act of writing presupposed certain material and cultural resources that Wright did not have access to in Mississippi. In response to Ellison's idealism, Howe commented that he shared with Wright an understanding that if authentic freedom was to be obtained, a person would have to leave the realm of the imagination. "A social action was required."[67] The exceptional Wright understood clearly that a meaningful freedom necessarily included the non-exceptional.

The attempt to invoke the exceptional person as the standard-bearer of possibility for the entire ethnic group is predicated on simultaneous reifications of the exceptional person and the not-so-exceptional ethnic group. That is, to designate someone representative of a group of persons is not only to create, isolate, and reify specific but ultimately arbitrary qualities that supposedly constitute the meaningful core of potentially shared group traits (that is, race, gender, or ethnicity) but also to employ these as the most significant indicators of the individual group member's human essence.[68] In making any individual black person representative of the possibilities for all blacks, Ellison writes as if blackness was the most crucial component of every Afro-American life.

This line of argument implies that the journey of Leontyne Price from Mississippi to Carnegie Hall supposedly has some connection with the quality of life of black stevedores on a Memphis dock. Ellison has long claimed that blacks were not distinctly black culturally but an amalgam of various American ethnic cultures. Whence comes therefore Ellison's willingness to designate a specific black as being representative of all blacks (that is, Richard Wright and Leontyne Price for black Mississippi)? Do class, gender, or even the variations in the quality of racism experienced by individual blacks inhibit such ethnic uniformity?

Ellison can only invoke the irony of the exceptional black by calling forth, affirming, and then subverting existing stereotypes of blacks (or existing social-science influenced perceptions of black typicalities). These social-scientific perceptions of blacks are for Ellison tantamount to stereotypes. He warns us to be on the lookout for the "little man at Chehaw station"[69] who will emerge from a crowd of faceless blacks when we least expect it, critically informed and demanding excellence. In so doing the little man will shatter our prefabricated perceptions of black Americans. The ironic intensity of various episodes with such little men depends on the depth of our stereotypes of blacks or the value that we place on social-scientific depictions of black uniformity.

Ellison's ontology of black life would have us believe that most, if not all, Negroes could be capable of functioning in some capacity in some arena like the little man at Chehaw Station. In this sense all Negroes violate accepted social-scientific categorizations of black people or racist stereotypes. Black life is as complex as any life. Oppression is not a great leveler. Black heroism abounds.

Insofar as Ellison's exceptional black exists in antagonistic cooperation with black stereotypes, it is a reified negation of a reified depiction. Ellison's exceptional Negro is far too predictable and always individualized by being not only unlike what we expect Negroes to be but actually unlike "the other Negroes." But is the state of being unlike other Negroes sufficiently exhaustive of human possibility? Ellison would probably answer that it is and, moreover, that such exceptional blacks are quite typical. As such, Ellison's exceptional Negro is not like the archetypal exceptional Negro. The archetypal exceptional Negro, based on the idea of the exceptional Jew in post-emancipated Europe, is a parvenu who bases his own advancement on his distinctiveness from other members of his ethnic group, who are deemed guilty of living in the stereotyped manner.[70] Ellison's exceptional blacks do not try to divorce themselves from their ethnic group, nor do they attempt to gain access to broader white society by reinforcing the stereotypes visited upon the black masses. Instead they are the standard-bearers of ethnic possibility and, by inversion, the representative black. They are heroic blacks.

Ellison's claim that Richard Wright became a successful novelist even though he grew up in Mississippi supposedly indicates both black Mississippi's freedom and Wright's exceptionalism. The latter leads us to conclude that Wright became a novelist despite growing up in Mississippi. The former leads us to say that Wright became a writer because he grew up in Mississippi. In the latter instance Wright is the representative of black possibility while in the former, Wright is the representative of blacks. Wright the exceptional Negro who violated numerous Afro-American mores and traditions in becoming a novelist becomes for Ellison comprehensible through an understanding of the traditions, hopes, and aspirations of Afro-Americans. A dialectical irony is at work.

In reifying Wright by turning him into objective proof of the humanity of the Negro living in brutally racist Mississippi, Ellison does not investigate below the surface of his critical assertion that Wright was too ideologically doctrinaire to describe black life in Mississippi honestly. If Ellison truly wanted to pursue his inquiry concerning Wright to its logical conclusion, he would have had to investigate why Mississippi produced in Richard Wright a novelist incapable of writing about the humanity of black people (using Ellison's definition of humanity). Ellison credits Mississippi for Wright's emergence as a novelist but denies Mississippi responsibility for the way in which Wright perceived the world and used the novel. Allison Davis has written that Wright hated and feared whites and despised blacks.[71] If true, might this too have to be considered part of the burden of growing up in Mississippi under such extreme conditions? Are these attitudes expressions of Wright's freedom in and/or from Mississippi? Contrary to Ellison's claims, Wright did not free himself in Mississippi. He possibly freed himself from Mississippi by physically leaving the state. Yet Wright never succeeded in freeing himself psychologically from Mississippi.[72]

It is almost too ironic that Ellison would conclude his dialogue with Howe by attempting to situate himself within the context of a political movement, the black civil rights struggle of the 1950s and 1960s. Howe had written, "If Ellison chooses not to participate directly in the Negro struggle but instead to stick by his work as a novelist, that is a decision I respect—though it seems neither unfriendly nor untruthful to say that it is perhaps a costly decision to make."[73] Ellison responded,

> Dear Irving, I am still yaking on and there's many a thousand gone, but I assure you that no Negroes are beating down my door, putting pressure on me to join the Negro Freedom Movement, for the simple reason that they realize that I am enlisted for the duration. Such pressure is coming only from a few disinterested "military advisers," since Negroes want no more fairly articulate would-be Negro leaders, cluttering up the airways. For you see, my Negro friends recognize a certain division of labor among the members of the tribe. Their demands, like that of many whites, are that I publish more novels—and here I am remiss and vulnerable perhaps.[74]

If only Ellison knew just how wrong his assertion would prove to be. Perhaps no major black intellectual had his door knocked on more often than Ralph Ellison precisely because he was viewed by some as having gone AWOL from the Negro freedom movement. Contrary to Ellison's claims, the division of labor existed in his head, not in the heads of the Negroes. Projecting his personal rationalizations onto a mass public, Ellison was attempting to tell Howe and others how they should interpret his disengaged behavior.

Some blacks who were involved in the civil rights movement, including numerous black intellectuals, were disappointed if not angered by Ellison's unwillingness to lend his talents openly to the cause. That anger surfaced during a 1965 conference of the American Society of African Culture on the black writer. Ellison was not in attendance. His political detachment from the Negro movement was subjected to severe criticism. Novelist John Oliver Killens, a longtime Ellison foe, and historian John Henrik Clarke were the primary protagonists. Harold Cruse transcribed the dialogue:

> John Henrik Clarke also got in his blows at Ellison:
> "I particularly wanted to take up with Mr. Hill this continued love affair with Ralph Ellison who is standing outside of his people's struggle, making olympian remarks about how that struggle should be conducted."
> Hill, who is the NAACP's Labor Secretary, replied:
> "I would categorically deny that, by the way. I am sorry that we don't have a chance to discuss Mr. Ellison's work. I would simply challenge that point of view."
> Clarke:
> "I hope Mr. Hill can be brief with this exaggeration of the role of Ralph Ellison who has spent so much time in the last ten years in flight from his own people and has not even answered most mail addressed to him by his fellow black writers and has said positively that art and literature are not racial. He won't come into any Afro-American writer's conference. I think Ellison wrote one very interesting thing. From the point of view of craftsmanship it was a very good and powerful work. Whether Ralph Ellison will follow up, whether Ralph Ellison has grown up is open to question in many quarters starting with me."[75]

Following another statement by Hill in defense of Ellison and a perfunctory statement of criticism by white Marxist historian Herbert Aptheker, Clarke added:

> I want to take the qualification further than that. I think Dr. Aptheker put it correctly. I was referring to the last ten years. And the last ten years when Baldwin took flight and went to Paris hating himself and his people, literally, but did come back and enter the mainstream of the struggle. Whether he is psychologically back home completely opens maybe a question. But at least he knows the road that leads to

home. But Mr. Ralph Ellison seems to have been going further away from home in that sense.[76]

As he had done in his debate with Howe, Ellison would undoubtedly have refuted any insinuation that he had ever ruptured his relationship with black America. Moreover, Ellison's notion of "home" would be different from that implied by John Henrik Clarke. He would never think of "coming home" under the terms insinuated by Clarke. Clarke essentially was calling for Ellison to enter an organic intellectual relationship with the politicized black populace, whereas Ellison cherished the solitude and distance of the traditional intellectual life. Unsurprisingly, Ellison would never ground his artistic legitimacy in terms of popular black acceptance. Sure, he wanted black readers, but he did not believe in following their political dictates. An elitist, Ellison did not take his cues from the masses. Ever the individualist, he would remain suspicious of political movements, particularly those that assumed a posture of incontestable morality. Certainly Ellison supported the civil rights movement, but he did not believe that he should function as a propagandist for that movement. The idea of being linked to a social or political movement is seen by Ellison as intrinsically dysfunctional to his artistic life.

Albert Murray captured the essence of Ellison's position: "No truly serious or truly dedicated writer can afford to enlist in any movement except on his own terms. The risks of arrogance which he runs by insisting on such politically suspect individuality are occupational hazards against which only his integrity can protect him. He must elect to be consistent with himself and suffer the consequences. . . . Other people can always hold the writer accountable for everything he does, of course; but he can allow no one to tell him what to write."[77]

Criticism from Killens and Clarke did not constitute definitive condemnation from the emerging civil rights movement. While these men were engaged as polemicists, speakers, and writers in behalf of the movement, their antagonism to Ellison may have stemmed from a different source. Insofar as Ellison had broken with the Left and had rejected socialist realism, he may have been targeted as an illegitimate black by these left-wing intellectuals. Cruse also suggests intellectual/artistic envy as a motive of the attacks.[78] Nevertheless, criticism from various sectors of the emerging black protest movement was directed toward

Ellison. As the civil rights movement splintered and the black power era arose, the criticisms of Ellison emanating from the black community became deafening at times. Such criticisms were not only directed at Ellison's disengaged political stance but also at his distinct, culturally pluralistic description of the Negro.

In an interpretation of the Howe-Ellison debate that was published in 1966, entitled "Ralph Ellison and the Uses of the Imagination," literary critic Robert Bone supported Ellison's claim for the autonomy of art.[79]

> It will be clear, I trust that I am speaking out of no hostility to the Freedom Movement or to politics as such. I am arguing not for the abandonment of militancy but for the autonomy of art. There is no need for literature and politics to be at odds. It is only when the aesthete approaches politics as if it were a poem, or when the political activist approaches the poem as if it were a leaflet, that the trouble starts. . . . Emerson distinguishes between the Doer and the Sayer and refuses to honor one at the expense of the other.[80]

Bone went on to say that Ellison was, in effect, engaged in the black freedom struggle in the only way that a writer knew.

> The Negro writer, who is surely not free of social responsibility must yet discharge it *in his own fashion*, which is not the way of politics but art; not the lecture platform but the novel and the poem. Without repudiating his sense of obligation to the group, Ellison has tried to express it through services which only the imagination can perform.
>
> What is at issue is the role of the imagination in that complex process which we call civilization. The visionary power, the power of naming, the power of revealing a people to itself are not to be despised. If those who can command these powers are diverted from their proper task, who will celebrate the values of the group, who create those myths and legends, those communal rites which alone endow the life of any group with meaning?[81]

Bone's response is a mixture of hyperbole and substance. Certainly he does not actually believe that the meaning of black existence would have been in doubt had Ellison or other black writers ceased to write. Bone's reply is as problematic as Ellison's response to Howe. Both men commodify and privilege the writer. No longer a person living in the world, the writer becomes a glorified entity associated with art production. Why, one may ask, is the writer devoid of the political responsibilities of the truck driver or the minister? The implication of Ellison's and Bone's defense of the apolitical artist is that the writer somehow has been endowed with a privileged disengagement from mundane matters of the world. Unsurprisingly, this privilege is not dependent on recognition from nonwriters. Bone's train of thought leads to the conclusion that there are professional political activists whose job is to protest. What else could Ellison have meant by a division of labor in the movement? If Ellison's only responsibility is to write more novels, then why is it not the teacher's only task to teach better or the businessman's sole task to expand his market and lower his prices? Had everyone continued to pursue their professional career or private interests, there would have been no civil rights movement.

Bone and Ellison refused to situate the writer materially within society. Had either done so, the writer would have become less of a mechanized conduit of universal values and more of a real, living person with material interests and the accompanying desires to articulate those peculiar interests as universally significant. Bone implies that those interested in politicizing Ellison demanded that he write propaganda. How could such statements be made in an era of Silone, Cesaire, Sartre, and de Beauvoir? There are numerous ways for artists to express themselves politically without placing their talents in the service of propaganda. To look at the writer's options for political expression in such narrow terms is to misunderstand what was most significant about Richard Wright. Instead of arguing that the responsibilities of the writer necessitate distance from political activity, Bone could have admitted that Ellison, like many other writers and nonwriters, is simply not a politically engaged person. Bone cannot make this claim for the same reason that Ellison does not make it. Both men feel that the black writer as a black is *supposed* to be engaged. Ellison wants us to accept his argument that apoliticization is the political engagement of the writer, provided, that is, that he or she is engaged in artistic production. A fighter fights and a writer writes.

Though a student and admirer of Afro-American folklore and folk art, Ellison does not consider himself a folk artist. Ellison appears to adhere to the enduring romantic distinction between folk art and fine art. In this view, "The art of the people [folk art] was something which grew organically and which was propagated according to an unbroken tradition, while the art of the cultured [fine art] was a conscious and planned experimental activity."[1] In folk art there is little if any distinction between producer and consumer. According to Arnold Hauser, the romantic theory of folk art holds to "the unity of the folk-spirit and emphasizes that traditional forms of art are the common property of the people and not the property of one particular class."[2]

Ellison believes that folk art and folklore hold the keys to understanding a people's existence. Through folklore a people comment on their worldly situation and historically revise the common lessons for survival that need to be passed from generation to generation. Within Afro-American folklore, "the values, styles and character types of black American life and culture are preserved and reflected in a highly energized, often very eloquent language."[3] Folklore, Ellison notes, is "the group's attempt to humanize the world."[4] He states, "In folklore we tell what Negro experience really is . . . with a complexity of vision that seldom gets into our writing. . . . We back away from the chaos of experience and from ourselves, we depict the humor as well as the horror of our lives."[5]

Echoing the assertion of Constance Rourke, whose writings significantly influenced him, Ellison asserts that "great literature is erected upon this humble base of folk forms."[6] In a praiseworthy study of folklore and American literary theory, *The Voice of the Folk*, Gene Bluestein commented on Ellison's claim: "It is precisely what folk ideologues have always argued: the authentic sources of a nation's culture lie in the lower levels and if they are developed sensitively, not only the poet speaks but his nation also finds its expression."[7]

Ellison views his mandate as a fine artist as a challenge not only to excel in his particular craft but to do so in such a way as to give expression to the voice of his folk. In order to master the particular craft in which Ellison sought to provide such expression, he has spent tremendous energy consciously studying and attempting to approximate the form and technique of the best works in his genre.

Ellison, the novelist as blues aestheticist, stated to the surprise of some that the fine literary artist (read novelist) "to achieve proper resonance, must go beyond the blues."[8] In *Blues, Ideology, and Afro-American Literature*, Houston Baker transcribed the following elaboration from a 1982 Ellison appearance on the BBC: "The blues are very important to me. I think of them as the closest approach to tragedy that we have in American art forms. And I'm not talking about black or white, I mean just American. Because they do combine the tragic and the comic in a very subtle way and, yes, they are very important to me. But they are also limited. And if you are going to write fiction there is a level of consciousness which you move toward which I would think transcends the blues."[9] Baker is somewhat troubled by Ellison's willingness to rank the value of folklore beneath that of fine literary art. Ultimately, Baker argues that "the distinction between folk-lore and literary art evident in Ellison's critical practice collapses in his creative practice in *Invisible Man*'s Trueblood episode."[10] Baker, in effect, rescues Ellison from himself, at least in Baker's eyes. In any case, Baker does not explore the utter centrality of Ellison's aesthetic romanticism to Ellison's entire intellectual/artistic project. It is the differentiation between folk art and fine art that allows Ellison to be simultaneously with the folk and divorced from them. As a fine artist, his artistic traditions and reference points are external to the folk. In fact, Ellison the fine artist is not and does not want to appear ethnically circumscribed. He is a participant in something far larger. As a fine artist who gives artistic value to his people's folklore, he seems decidedly with the ethnic group. Ironically, one of the most intellectually and artistically elitist black artists of his generation, Ellison is regarded by some black critics as a populist-oriented, black cultural nationalist.

Needless to say, it is not the nation that determines whether the poet spoke appropriately in its behalf. Folk ideology is an ideology of nonfolk artists that attempts to mask the significant gulf between the folk and the fine artist. The class distinctions did not go unrecognized by Hauser: "We can talk of folk-art only when class and cultural differences exist and only in antithesis to the art of nonpopular strata. Folk-art is not a communal art but—like artistic production in general—a class or caste art."[11] Unlike Hauser, Ellison does not situate folk culture within a class context. Instead, he views Afro-American folk culture as the universal creation of all black Americans. Nevertheless, Afro-American folk culture is not the property of black Americans solely. It is rich, raw material lying in wait for all American fine artists who perceive and respect its profundity. White artists like Mark Twain who utilize Afro-American folk cultural motifs implicitly testify to the centrality of Afro-Americans to the American experience. However, in neglecting the caste/class nature of Afro-American folk culture, Ellison's formulation sidesteps having to confront the crucial distinction between those blacks who live within an Afro-American folk culture and those like himself who appropriate it consciously and eclectically for their own highbrow artistic ambitions. By ethnically reifying Afro-American folk culture, Ellison was able to mask the fact that he was not organically linked to all blacks. Ellison did not want to appear as appropriating Afro-American folk culture as an interloper, even though he does not actually frown on such appropriation by respectful white artists.

The sociopolitical implications of Ellison's invocation of a folk culture ideology inspired by Constance Rourke are profound. Rourke obtained much of her theory of folk culture from the writings of Johann Gottfried Herder, the eighteenth-century German philosopher.[12] According to Rourke, Herder provided folk expression with its most significant intellectual defense. Herder's work reveals some of the implications of Ellison's approach to culture.

In his study of the intellectual precursors of modern anthropological conceptions of culture, J. Q. Merquior allots a prominent position to Herder's historicism. (This is not the historicism of Karl Popper, which centers around predictability).[13] Merquior, borrowing from Donald Kelly's *Foundations of Modern Historical Scholarship*, viewed historicism (including Herder's) as the "search not for the typical but for the unique in history—a change-minded quest that emphasizes the variety rather than the uniformity of human nature and is interested less in similarities than in differences."[14] Herein may lie some of the theoretical origins of Ellison's celebration of the exceptional individual as the representative individual.

Merquior attributes to Herder the detachment of an idea of culture from the idea of civilization. In so doing, Herder helped to undermine the original evaluative sense of the two concepts that had referred to "a progressive quality of both the material and the moral states of mankind as a whole."[15] He succeeded in replacing the former ideas with an idea of "the incommensurability of different cultural wholes."[16]

Herder developed a formal philosophy of history that viewed history as moving in a circular fashion.

The leveling implications of such a cyclic view prevailed over the original value laden propensity of historicism.

. . . Historicism could only conceive of cultures, in the plural; in the singular, culture was always, to a historicist mind, preceded by an indefinite article emphasizing the plurality, the essential diversity of cultures along ethnic lines. . . . A singular, *hierarchical* idea of culture gave way to an essentially plural, *differential* one. The sense of superiority in *unitarianism* began to be challenged by an egalitarian awareness of *uniqueness*. . . . Thus the pluralistic neutrality vis-à-vis cultural particularism, professed by the historicist mind, heralded that "deevaluativization" of the culture concept, without which anthropology, as an empirical social science, could not have been born.

. . . Herder qualifies as the chief creator of the belief that human variety is bound to exist and is in itself an invaluable thing. He turned the expressiveness of nationhood, instead of the perfectibility of the individual into the core of culture.[17]

In appropriating an antitheoretical Herder through Constance Rourke's *American Humor* (1931) and *The Roots of American Culture* (1942), Ellison also appropriated Rourke's naive understanding of the implication of such nationalistic thinking. Historicism would eventually deny individuality through its development of an "oversocialized conception of culture."[18] Merquior clarifies this point:

When historicism did away with the normative, pedagogic concept of culture, it also cast a shadow on one important aspect of the humanist idea; its concern with humanity as a function of the individual person. The living subject of paideia, humanitas, or Bildung was in effect always an individual; but in the holism inherent in the historicist culture concept, the notion of culture as an individual attribute scarcely survived.

It is not that historicist historians . . . dislike individuality. On the contrary . . . they profess a sincere fondness of historical or cultural uniqueness; but mark: the individuals they so respect and exalt, jealously guarding them against subsumption under the typical or general *are always collective wholes.* True historicists historians have more often than not little love for the socially divisive potential of class and personality: *they think in terms of nations and ages, never of persons and classes.* . . . *Historicists may like individuality: yet, as good holists, they feel no affection towards individualism.*[19]

Ellison embodies modern-day intellectual historicist tendencies. He views the folk as an artistically undifferentiated mass, though he assigns to the folk the task of generating culture. Yet in mastering a high art, it is the fine artist, not the folk artist, who has differentiated himself from the folk and realized his individuality.[20] Artistic self-consciousness is the crucial precondition for the would-be fine artist. In realizing his or her individuality, the fine artist gives the folk a lasting identity. Whether the folk would view Ellison as their spokesperson or as someone who should be offering them "equipment for living" is open to question.

Insofar as the Herder-influenced Ellison views black Americans as creators of a folk culture as rich as any other folk tradition, black intellectuals have often celebrated him for articulating a black cultural nationalist perspective.[21] He clearly valued Afro-American culture. Yet, it is not at all clear the degree to which Ellison intrinsically valued the black people who were carriers of this tradition. Instead, he occasionally appears to write as if these people were significant precisely because they provided him, the fine artist, with the humble base on which to build his unique fine artistic creations. Ellison's elitism was grounded in his aesthetics.

Had Ellison been more concerned about the folk and less concerned about the folklore they produced, he may not have been so quick to romanticize Afro-American folklore, for there is a great deal of black folklore and folk culture that is vulgar, despicable, and destructive to black people. Ellison's folk pastoralism celebrates blacks for singing the blues and creating jazz, but he concertedly overlooks those aspects of the black folk culture that view it as a source of pride to pistol-whip women, to kill someone in a cold-blooded manner, to father numerous children without concern for their upbringing, or to pimp women. In *Black Literature in White America*, German literary critic Berndt Ostendorf has perceptively stated,

> The materials of folklore cannot be divorced from the social and political context in which they arose. Thus the oral tradition is bound up with disenfranchisement, illiteracy and bondage; conversely, black folklore also stores fantasies and dreams, harbors that populist cussedness, so typical of all folklore and counsels strategies of survival in an oppressive world. Depending on the situation in which it is put to use it may be reactionary or progressive, escapist or rebellious.... The

charge may be made, and has been made, that Ellison counsels reconciliation with the problem-solving strategies of black folklore. . . .

. . . It is perhaps easier to celebrate that which does not enslave you, and indeed here are hints of pastoralism in his [Ellison's] urban appreciation of rural folklore.[22]

Ellison appears at times to be out of touch with contemporary Afro-America, for he writes/speaks as if Harlem is alive with blacks who sing the blues or dance to jazz bands. Today most blacks are subjected to popular culture. Mass-marketed artifacts such as Janet Jackson, Grover Washington, Michael Jackson, Bill Cosby, and Mr. T. have very little to do with a distinct organic, ethnic folk culture, theirs or anyone's.[23] Not only does Ellison romanticize Afro-American folk culture, weeding out arbitrarily that which he does not like, but his notion of folk culture also stands outside time and social influences.[24] When Ellison talks about folk culture, he really means folk culture artifacts. Insofar as the folk are no longer immersed in folk cultures but in mass culture at worst, pop culture at best, Ellison cannot now claim to derive his fine art forms from contemporary black folk, unless he wants to temper his claim to providing the world with an ethnically peculiar voice. Divorced from the folk, Ellison was able to treat them merely as living depositories of a timeless ethnic folk culture. His conception is a folk culture frozen in time and divorced from the living folks. As such it can continue to exist indefinitely.

From Ellison's beliefs about folk culture and the folk, it follows that his notion of democracy is a notion of cultural pluralism. His view appears democratic, for it respects the voice of each group. America is democratic precisely because it is made up of numerous cultural voices. His vision is highly antidemocratic insofar as within each group only the fine artists can convey the group's collective voice and they do so without having to obtain the group's consent. His views are premised on problematic reifications and, as such, hide various types of intraethnic group cleavages and assume as a rational given the primacy of an individual artist's allegiance to ethnic, national, or racial groupings.

Ellison's willingness to ignore the sociopolitical lives of black individuals for the sake of the group's cultural voice was displayed in his speech at Bank Street College.

And consider this; one of the most influential musicians to come out of Oklahoma was a gifted boy who never took part in school musical activities (and ours was a musically oriented Negro community) because he was considered "lower class" in his attitudes. I refer to Charlie Christian, the jazz guitarist, who accomplished that rare feat of discovering the jazz idiom, the jazz voice, of a classical instrument. And yet, here was a child who lived in a hotbed of everything that middle-class people fear—the tuberculosis rate was sky-high, crime, prostitution, bootlegging, illness. There was all of the disintegration which you find among rural Negroes who are pounding themselves to death against the sharp edges of an urban environment. Yet this was one of the most wonderful places I've even known. Here imagination was freely exercised by the kids. They made toys. They made and taught themselves to play musical instruments. They lived near the city dump, and they converted the treasures which they found there to their own uses. This was an alive community in which the harshness of slum life was inescapable but in which the strength, the imagination of the people, was much in evidence. And yet you would have to say that it was indeed lower class, and lower-lower class, and according to the sociologists utterly hopeless. Certainly it was no place to search for good minds or fine talent.

But how many geniuses do you get anywhere? And where do you find a first class imagination? Who really knows. Imagination is where you find it; thus we must search the whole scene. Oh, but how many pretentious little kids have we been able to develop through progressive education! We can turn out a hell of a lot of these.[25]

Ellison is rhetorically willing to silence the pain and desperateness of Charlie Christian and his poor neighbors simply because of Christian's musical genius that evidently gave these people their voice. His concern is less with the folk than with the artistic production of the heroic individual who comes out of the folk and renders their suffering meaningful. Amidst the chaos of poor black life, Christian developed a love for music and an artistic discipline that allowed him to hone his craft into a fine art form. If a middle-class white community was to produce only one genius, then on what grounds can we claim that economically impoverished black life was in any way more culturally deprived than the middle-class white life? Therein lies the key to Ellison's belief that the exceptional individual carries the identity of the group. Ellison celebrates Christian, the heroic artist who transcended his surroundings to play jazz guitar for the Benny Goodman Orchestra. Yet this celebration comes at the cost of ignoring the plight of the nonheroic individuals who comprised the majority of the community in which Christian was raised. Ellison might reply that those supposedly nonheroic, poor, black Oklahoma City dwellers did comprise a heroic collective, for they were instrumental in retaining and nurturing a folk music form that gave rise to and cultivated Christian's individual artistic quest.

The roots of Ellison's philosophy in Herder lead to an understanding of why he would never openly and explicitly pursue social marginality. Simply put, Ellison could never openly isolate himself from black America precisely because his authentic aesthetic identity would be at stake. To divorce himself from blacks, that is, black folk culture, would be to deny himself the raw materials that he needs to construct fine Afro-American art. Furthermore, the historicism of Herder through Rourke allows Ellison as a fine artist to differentiate himself psychologically from the ethnic group in order to practice his craft while appearing to remain grounded in the folk culture. He can utilize the folk culture without being with the folk. It is an elitist nationalist vision, one that renders the everyday world of black people less significant than the way that they dance, hum, or play basketball.

Ellison has often been misinterpreted by black nationalists as a kindred spirit. Insofar as he celebrates black folk culture, he appears sympathetic to black cultural nationalism, but Ellison is not a black nationalist. He is a Negro nationalist and insofar as he believes that Negro culture is an American phenomenon and occupies a centrality within American culture, Ellison is an American nationalist. While he believes in being linked to black folk, he does not believe that blacks' culture is culturally black. He believes that blacks are culturally part Irish, part Italian, part Jewish, and vice versa. Blacks have been seminal creators of American culture, and America has been a profound influence on the creation of black culture. In effect, black and white Americans have lived in antagonistic cooperation.

Unlike Wright, who pursued the life of an outsider, Ellison wanted to plant himself as deeply in the core of American culture as possible and does so by arguing for the centrality of Afro-American folk culture to American culture. While Wright underestimated the significance of his mainstream American cultural identity as a Negro, Ellison underestimated the significance of blacks as political and social outsiders regardless of cultural similarities with whites.[26] Politics meant everything to Wright. Culture means everything to Ellison. In crucial respects, Geoffrey Hartman's description of Malraux could easily apply to Ellison: "His views have changed in accord with the principle that politics should serve culture rather than culture politics."[27]

Ellison's confrontation with the victim status is subtle and quite unique. He neither attempts to scare whites with images of brute Negroes, like Wright, nor does he champion an image of blacks as morally superior beings, like Baldwin. Ellison claims to be the black writer who is less concerned with appealing to whites than in creating art that affirms black life. Yet one of the major manifestations of Ellison's entrapment in the black victim status lies in his consistent hesitancy to confront the fact that black Americans have been profoundly adversely affected by their subjugation in America. In his public statements Ellison will sometimes offer a perfunctory mention of the dire plight of many blacks before he proceeds into a celebration of black American creative endurance and American possibility. According to Ellison, descriptions of blacks that assert the existence of a "mark of oppression" implicitly deny the humanity of blacks. Ellison utilizes hegemonic American democratic rhetorics as well as the resilient hopeful outlooks of many black Americans to divert his attention from the most debilitating aspects of black existence in America. At times he appears to live in a fantasy of the healthy black adaptation to an oppressive environment, an adaptation that has as its metaphor, the blues. Would Bigger Thomas's life have been less destitute had he loved the blues? Perhaps, but not necessarily so. The despair, hopelessness, and anomie experienced by large sectors of the black urban populace today are not the by-products of the absence of an urban black cultural agency. Instead, they are the result of a sustained, systematic denial of opportunity, both perceived and real.[28]

Ellison does not ignore racial oppression in America. However, his ideological perspective limits his ability to perceive the depth of the impact of subjugation in people's lives. Ellison's ideology borders on a celebration of a therapeutic "escape from freedom" as opposed to real freedom. He implies that if a subjugated people feel good about themselves, their situation is not desperate. Self-affirmation supposedly keeps the harshest aspects of the oppressive wolf from the door. Folk tales that keep dreams of opportunity alive are posited as antidotes to the absence of real opportunity. Such ideas led Ellison to claim that Wright freed himself in Mississippi. It even leads Ellison to make inane claims such as instead of freedom the slaves had folklore.[29] Free or unfree, blacks had folklore. Reciting folk tales in the slave cabin embodies only a very partial negation of one's status as slave. Ellison and his defenders might respond that during slavery black folklore was a counterhegemonic repository insofar as it helped the slaves to sustain a sense of their humanity in the face of a system that attempted at times to reduce them to property. Ellison's understanding of folklore as the repository of black self-affirmation in some ways prefigures the recent James Scott discussions about the significance of "hidden transcripts."[30] While hidden transcripts and other "weapons of the weak" are important, we must be careful not to view these as antidotes to exploitative dominance. Cursing the master under one's breath or participating in the ring shout did not ameliorate the naked power aspects of slave exploitation. That is, folklore may have helped some slaves to soothe some of the pain of "natal alienation," but it did nothing to halt the phenomenon.[31]

Though Ellison has repeatedly claimed that he is not concerned with proving the humanity of blacks, he repeatedly engages in this task. This is not a condemnation of Ellison. All artists in some way affirm and testify to humanity. Because Ellison views cultural production as the key to a people's humanity, he remains intent on proving that Afro-American culture is as diverse, rich, and complex as any people's culture. Insofar as the fine artist gives a proper voice to a people's culture, Ellison's task as a black writer is nothing less than securing for blacks an exalted place within the hierarchy of fine literature and, ultimately, substantiating their legitimacy as a people. Fine artists, however necessarily individualized, can carry explicit and implicit burdens and responsibilities far beyond themselves.

Through the invocation of the exceptional individual (à la the fine artist as opposed to the folk artist), Ellison embraces and celebrates heroic individualism.[32] Ellison is a dogmatic individualist, one who believes that the high points of human artistic creativity are, ultimately, individual affairs. As an individual fine artist, Ellison believes that he can speak to and in behalf of black Americans. He might argue that the value of his fictional representation of blacks is determined in large measure by the degree to which he, a fine artist, assumes the tortuous burden of disciplining his mind, respecting his subject matter, and perfecting his craft. Most persons are neither up to the task creatively nor capable of enduring the psychological demons that accompany serious artistic engagement.

Heroic individualists, like most ambitious fine artists, are not fundamentally democratically minded. They may espouse democratic ideology, but they tend to view themselves as a select group, select by virtue of talent but more importantly by virtue of their sheer artistic willpower and bravery. Most do not hear the call, but still fewer answer it. Heroic individualists tend to view the good in the world as having been shaped by other heroic individuals. Ellison's fondness for heroic individualism may have led him to view the blues as the embodiment of an existentialist philosophy of life. Such feelings may have been further reinforced by Ellison's reading of Miguel de Unamuno's *The Tragic Sense of Life*, a text in which heroism is explicitly celebrated.[33] Ellison claims to have been influenced by the Unamuno text. In commenting on Unamuno's concept of the heroic, Victor Ouimette writes, "Peace and happiness form no part of the goals, for the hero must reveal the misery and emptiness of the average man, dynamically and painfully. He will always have the feeling of crying in the wilderness, no matter how concrete and specific his human objectives may be. However, this is, once again, why it is necessary for him to be both slightly callous and prepared to appear, ridiculous without fear. This is the torment of the mission and the price of eternity."[34] Ellison celebrates the blues as a creative art form, but he does not view the blues as having set the artistic standard for him to match or exceed. His mission is far beyond the blues. In his willingness to confront the "price of eternity," Ellison views himself in "antagonistic cooperation" with his artistic heroes of the past: Twain, Hemingway, Dostoyevsky, Faulkner, Joyce, and Eliot. These ambitions, which must be kept secret, may have fueled in Ellison a sense of insult and disgust at Irving Howe's attempt to place him on an artistic playing field with Richard Wright. Ellison's ambitions not only exceeded Wright's, but the ambitions that Howe attributed to all black writers. Equally important, but lost in the polemical shuffle, Ellison's intellectual and artistic ambitions may have exceeded Howe himself. Of course, the latter possibility probably did not dawn on Howe or on most readers of the debate.

While Ellison represents blacks in his fiction, actual living blacks have little if any direct influence over what Ellison does or does not do. The heroic individualist conspicuously attempts to maintain no personal obligations to living people that are not initiated by the heroic individual himself. Ellison would always be suspicious of organizations and collectives. When told that novelist Leon Forrest had stated that Forrest, Toni Morrison, Albert Murray, James McPherson, and Ralph Ellison constituted a "crowd" of similar writers, Ellison respectfully dissented:

> It's an interesting grouping for writers whom I respect; still I am by instinct (and experience) a loner. There is no question . . . that we share what Malraux has termed a "collectivity of sensibilities." . . . But as to our constituting a school, that kind of thing—no. I don't think it desirable even though it offers one relief from the loneliness of the trade. For when writers associate too closely there is a tendency to control one another's ideas. I'm not implying that association is itself necessarily a negative matter, but I suspect that the loneliness of writing causes us to seek for a kind of certainty among our peers—when very often it's the *uncertainty* of the creative process which leads to new insights and to unanticipated formulation.[35]

Heroic individualists do not take their cues from the masses. They may align themselves with a group or mass public, but only when they chose to do it and always on their own terms. This lack of public obligation does not mean that the hero does not feel responsibility toward other people. It simply means that the hero is *never* forced to act. He or she simply chooses to do so. The absence of public obligation on the part of the hero can generate anger in those who believe that obligation should govern the hero's behavior.

During the past twenty (and perhaps thirty) years, Ellison has not publicly been part of any organized black intellectual effort to confront racist practices in American intellectual life. Other black intellectuals have asked him to use his enormous prestige in this effort, but to no avail. To engage in such a collective political effort would necessitate making alliances with black artists/intellectuals that Ellison deems to be his artistic (read personal) inferiors. In order not to have his status lowered by association with nonheroic blacks or to become entangled with mundane obligations, Ellison sidesteps such public engagement. However, Ellison has not opposed such efforts. Furthermore, he is willing to struggle in behalf of black artistic recognition in his own individual and private way.[36] Nevertheless, he at times tries to rationalize his public absence through a series of specious claims ("No one is knocking on my door"). When pushed, Ellison will simply admit that he believes that his only duty is to write. The writer, he would argue, should not be expected to join the picket line. Ellison might also argue that the artist does not belong on the picket line. Though heroic individualists tend to view themselves and their creative output through a collective recall of individual heroic fine artists who preceded them as well as envisioning those who will follow, the hero needs the group to validate his achievement. In addition, the hero believes that his individual struggle will benefit the group. Heroes are simultaneously part of and divorced from the group. If they merely mimic the group, they will cease to realize their heroic calling.

Ellison believes that social and political engagement may be antithetical to his artistic pursuit. He does not claim that all writers or even all black writers have to follow his particular example, though one does get the impression that hidden behind his professed tolerance for other intellectual styles is a belief that his own style is best for all serious writers.[37] Given the plight of blacks in America, politicized, socially conscious black writers could spend their entire day, every day of their lives, writing responses to some racist or racially parochial depiction of blacks carried in a local journal or newspaper. How does Ellison keep such demands at bay? Baldwin could not and thus answered the call of the civil rights movement. Ellison did not answer that call and continued to write his second novel.

In many respects, it is Langston Hughes and not Baldwin who represents the polar opposite of Ellison. In reading Rampersad's biography of Hughes, I was struck by the almost manic public intellectual life of Hughes. In effect, Hughes was too busy to write well. He would read to schoolchildren, attend every black person's opening night, write encouraging book reviews, appear on radio talk shows, and try to broker young black writers into print. Hughes was a literal one-man black intellectual infrastructure. Moreover, Hughes understood the value of being a public intellectual. In some respects, Hughes paid a terrible price for his generosity, for he was never able to hone his craft sufficiently. Excelling at writing took more energy and solitude than Hughes was willing or capable of enduring. Interestingly, the value of Hughes's contribution to the development of an Afro-American intellectual community will always be underrecognized in large part because those who study him may not appreciate the importance of the public intellectual life.

Ellison is not nearly as generous with his time. Moreover, he does not grant public intellectual life the same importance as does Hughes. Perhaps Ellison has always known that he could not write the way he aspires to and at the same time spend a great deal of time at public and political gatherings. When questioned about the political demands placed on the black writer, James Baldwin once admitted that he found these demands in conflict with the space he needed in order to write. Baldwin claimed that when he wanted to engage in serious writing, he would physically leave the United States. Baldwin said:

> In order to write you have to sit down and concentrate on that. Which means you've got to turn your back on everything else. It is impossible to do that in the situation in this country now. . . .
>
> For me it was necessary to move out so that I could see it because you don't see a situation very clearly when you're in it. You can't. You spend all of your time reacting to it, resisting it or resenting it, but you are not able to obtain any distance from it. Everything is too urgent. It is a matter of life or death. You must react everyday to what is happening. But that is no way to write a book or a sentence.[38]

Ellison did not physically relocate to another land, but his disengaged intellectual style may have been a necessary form of psychological immigration from the overbearing time commitments and psychological demands that accompany a politically engaged black intellectual existence in America. Ellison's willingness and ability to create a world of healthy black adaptation to subjugation may be nothing less than an attempt to fashion an image of the world that morally legitimates his political disengagement. It is, perhaps, a guilt-reducing fiction.

There are probably an infinite variety of black intellectual and artistic styles that occupy a middle ground between the hypergenerosity of

Hughes and the public stinginess of Ellison. Not only Baldwin, but Lorraine Hansberry, Ishmael Reed, Alice Walker, and Amiri Baraka immediately come to mind as occupying this middle ground. Of contemporary black writers, Maya Angelou appears most like Hughes in her generosity toward other black artists. Yet, to even mention the above writers as if they belong in the artistic company of Ellison will appear sacrilegious to Ellison's devotees and perhaps to Ellison himself. They might claim that all of the above should have spent more time writing and revising and less time engaging in political and social activities. Who knows—these critics might be correct. But they may be wrong. The catch-22 of heroic individualism is its hypercompetitiveness, a tendency to put down all of one's intellectual peers who answer a different call. Not everyone can be or wants to be a hero. Some heroes are not interested in individual recognition.

As a heroic individualist, Ellison appears to be tormented by his ambitions. The Achilles' heel of heroic individualism is unrealistic, almost obsessive-compulsive, artistic ambition. In such a mental state, one not only strives for perfection but perceives anything less as defeat or weakness. Certainly, there is something tragically obsessive-compulsive about Ellison spending forty years writing a second novel. On the other hand, individual artists like Ellison who have unrealizable expectations often succeed in ways far superior to those who entertain more easily realizable ambitions.

The importance of Ellison's example and intellectual style for the Afro-American intellectual community is that he calls blacks to a commitment to artistic/intellectual excellence. An equally important corollary to this call to excellence is that Ellison's intellectual style embodies and protects the fundamental freedom of the black artist and intellectual to be an artist/intellectual without apology.

In a besieged community, like Afro-America, intellectual activity often assumes a utilitarian ethic. Black intellectuals and artists who seek to explore their creative talents and interests, wherever they lead, often appear to be divorced from the needs of the community. Conversely, the black intellectual who spends time trying to decipher Rousseau's general will is vulnerable to attacks for being irrelevant, bourgeois, and self-centered. There is no adequate defense against such attacks. All artists create out of a love for their art form. They may, at times, place their talents in the service of a cause, but there can be no hiding from the fact that even when this is done, artists derive aesthetic pleasures in the creative act. Keeping in mind the self-interested core that lies at the root of artistic creation, one might conclude that the ambitious, artistic, or intellectual life might very well be irrelevant to the immediate or even long-term needs of a black community suffering the pangs of American economic, gender, and racial oppression.

She who derives pleasure from the study of slavery in the antebellum South may have little to contribute to the contemporary struggle for black emancipation. In creating a collage, Romare Bearden knew that he was not feeding hungry children in Harlem. As for being bourgeois, the ambitious artistic/intellectual life is most easily facilitated when one's stomach is not empty and the rent has been paid. Certainly there is an element of self-centeredness in any ambitious intellectual or artist. Could it be otherwise? Ellison's example, however extreme in its social and political disengagement, defends for black intellectuals and artists the right to and necessity of a commitment to the solitary life, discipline, and seriousness of purpose that is so much a part of the individual creative enterprise. For living this truth, he has often been condemned.

What would the history of black music have been had Louis Armstrong or Duke Ellington spent enormous amounts of time and energy on picket lines protesting the racism they had to confront as American jazz musicians? Might their music have suffered? Might their music have benefited from the better treatment they may have received as a result of walking picket lines? In response to these questions, Ellison might claim that instead of joining the picket line, Armstrong, Ellington, and others protested through their art form. In this argument, heroism supposedly lies in the fact that black jazz musicians were not sidetracked by white racist club owners and critics into devaluing their own artistic gifts. Yet, it would be naive to insinuate that these men ultimately received better treatment because of their musical skills. Someone had to engage in the concerted struggle to improve the status of jazz musicians in the United States before certain types of recognition and respect were granted to these excellent artists. Who were these people? The mere fact that we remember the names of stellar jazz musicians but do not readily know the names of those individuals who openly fought to improve the status of jazz is in part why Ellison's disengaged intellectual style is so seductive, particularly to traditional intellectuals and fine artists. In the end, it appears as if only those persons who individually excel creatively are given any recognition. Those black intellectuals/artists who may have sacrificed some of their creative time and energy in expanding the artistic opportunities for other blacks are forgotten or dismissed as minor. Is Langston Hughes not an example of this? It is here that the fundamental weaknesses in Ellison's heroic individualistic intellectual style are exposed. By severely downplaying the importance of political engagement as a necessary prelude to artistic opportunity, Ellison works under the myth that talent is naturally and inevitably recognized. Concerning black writers of the 1960s, he stated, "When the work of Negro writers has been rejected they have all too often protected their egos by blaming racial discrimination, while turning away from the fairly obvious fact that good art—and Negro musicians are ever present to demonstrate this— commands attention of itself, whatever the writer's politics or point of view. And they forget that publishers will publish almost anything which is written with even a minimum of competency."[39] This statement thoroughly misrepresented the realities of black musicians and writers. Either Ellison was fundamentally ignorant of issues confronting black artists/intellectuals or he was engaged in a concerted distortion. Given his acute mind, I suspect the latter was the case. After all, Ellison had to know that even the very best black jazz musicians were not commanding the attention of prominent, well-endowed foundations. Universities were certainly not overwhelming black jazz musicians with invitations to join the ranks of their faculty.[40] The broader American public was celebrating neither these musicians nor their music.

Moreover, black writers were often denied opportunities to publish because of racism. It had long been known that major commercial publishers did not want to be seen as having published too many books by blacks.[41] Once published, black authors were often financially exploited. Might Ellison have known that his old buddy Chester Himes was not receiving just compensation for his published books?

Why would Ellison make such an insensitive and utterly unnecessary statement?

On one hand, such statements could stem from the hypercompetitiveness that appears to be a result of Ellison's obsessive-compulsive intellectual style. It is a way for Ellison to say to those black writers who are having difficulty finding publishers that their craftsmanship is not even minimally competent. Another possibility (which is related to the first) is that Ellison makes such statements in part because of his dogmatic adherence to a rather doctrinaire establishmentarian American ideology. Ellison, a meritocratic elitist, believes that the American democratic ideals and constitutional form of government also share and attempt to protect the values of individual achievement. Because of his meritocratic elitism, Ellison has a vested interest in proclaiming failure and success as individual phenomena. Evidence of racism's impact on the assessment and acceptance of individual black achievement undermines Ellison's confusion of American ideals with American racial realities. Still, it must have been difficult for Ellison in 1963–64 to write as if blacks in the United States had begun to be treated in a meritocratic manner. In effect, Ellison was arguing either (1) that race relations in the United States had reached the point at which black musicians and writers were ultimately judged by the quality of their creativity or (2) that despite the fact that race relations were deeply problematic, black musicians and writers were given recognition for their talents. Both possibilities seem grossly incorrect.

However, should the United States ever advance to the point at which black jazz musicians and writers are given just recognition for their accomplishments, it will be the result of some type of political agitation. A sociopolitical struggle had to lay the groundwork for the possibility of black artistic recognition. In other words, traditional black intellectual activity may be created on the individual level, but it does not arrive in print or on stage without a preceding communal struggle. As a black academic teaching at an elite, predominantly white college, I can divorce myself from the struggles and problems of contemporary black America during the process of writing this book. However, I cannot claim that the intellectual space that I now occupy which allows me the time and peace of mind to engage in this privativistic activity is the result of a recognition of my talent alone. After all, my opportunity to have this job is a result of previous struggles that some blacks and whites engaged in to open the doors of elite white academia to black persons such as myself. The social preconditions for my intellectual life are definitely beyond the power of my individual will or talent. Once granted opportunity, the result is mine alone, but even then only metaphorically. In concentrating on the ideational qualities of intellectual and artistic production and ignoring the materiality of intellectual life, Ellison sidesteps a confrontation with some of the most serious problems and issues facing the black intelligentsia. Issues facing the black intelligentsia do not center merely around the perfection of individual artistic craft but around gaining access to the educational and financial resources that facilitate an individual pursuit of artistic betterment.

In retreating from explicit social and political engagement, Ellison attempts to avoid many of the most debilitating tensions confronting black intellectuals. It now appears striking that when interviewed Ellison is rarely asked about this by his interviewers.[42] It may be that the exaggerated aspects of Ellison's disengagement are rarely discussed because the primary interpreters of Ellison, academic literary critics, are themselves often disengaged from public intellectual activity.

One of the fascinating things about Ellison is his ability to mask his hyperindividuality through his invocation of folk culture and the blues. It is almost as if his mere mention of the blues as a crucial influence on his work inspires some literary critics to imagine him in some type of organic relationship with black blues folk audiences and artists.

Ellison's attempted resolution of the Afro-American victim status is quite ingenious. First, as a heroic individualist, Ellison's artistic self-definition was such that he did not assume the ideological identity angsts of hegemonic victim status discourses. In some sense, he simply stood above the fray, positing himself in an antagonistic cooperative relationship with all other heroic individualistic artists who stood above the mundane frays of their times. It appears ludicrous to even imagine a black like the elitist, arrogant Ellison appealing to a white man for validation of his black life.[43]

Second, by invoking a blues ontology, Ellison was able to define the plight of blacks as a universal human agon in which all oppressions are relativized. Whites did not escape life's turmoils and traumas in Ellison's worldview. Like blacks, they were caught in universal human struggles to realize their humanity. Though whites were not victimized by American racism, they had fundamental human conundrums to confront and transcend. The only difference was that their playing field was dissimilar to that of most blacks. However, whites were not more heroic than blacks, nor did "white culture" stimulate more heroism than "black culture."

Furthermore, whites did not have any greater insight into confronting and transcending human dilemmas. Ellison steps outside the black victim status by the very fact that he defines fine artistic achievement and heroic activity in individualistic terms and thus eliminates and undermines comparative group dialogues.

It is not clear whether Ellison has successfully navigated the Afro-American victim status in all of its myriad guises. As stated earlier, he appears to have succeeded in transcending some variations of the black victim status syndrome while being unable to escape the lures of other forms of the victim status. However, Ellison's decision to envelop himself in an intensified elitist individuality as a social marginality facilitator appears to have been an outright artistic failure. That is, the choice made by Ellison to utilize elitist individualism as a mechanism for protecting and nurturing his creativity and viability as a writer does not appear to have worked. Whereas Baldwin retreated to Europe occasionally and Wright permanently, Ellison permanently retreated to the elitism of heroic individualism. Ellison has stated that Wright's decision to venture to Europe was disastrous for his writing. According to this argument, expatriation failed Wright as a social marginality facilitator. But has Ellison fared any better? Has his journey into the elitism of heroic individualism been any more artistically productive than Wright's flight to France? Whether or not Ellison ever publishes a stellar second or third novel, his forty-year effort to do so seems to indicate a creative failure of sorts. One issue that all artists and intellectuals must confront is how to develop an intellectual style that generates ambitions sufficiently grand to stimulate creativity but not so grand as to stifle it. It might well be the case that Ellison's outlandish ambitions have suffocated him artistically. If this is true, Ellison did not utilize a social marginality facilitator appropriate to his needs.

These suffocating ambitions may be by-products of racism. Suppose, for instance, that Ellison's ambitions stem from a need to prove himself in the eyes of white writers or the Western literati at large. The task of completing a writing project becomes increasingly difficult to the degree that Ellison inflates the greatness of those master white writers with whom he competes. While Ellison may display a unique version of this phenomenon, this is a rather typical black intellectual "disease." It is a disease that arises out of the struggle to confront the inevitable internalization of inferiority among subjugated persons. As such it is not merely a black intellectual disease but a mind-set found among colonized and subjugated intellectuals throughout the world. It is a psychological mind-set that generates a suffocating, debilitating desire to prove oneself either capable or superior, depending on the depth of one's insecurity and the quality of one's perceived talents. The real problem arises when this black intellectual creates a fictitious white standard-bearer that he cannot possibly measure up to or satisfy. No one, white or black, could measure up to it. In effect, the black intellectual governed by this particular neurosis is programmed not to realize his or her authentic talents. In this sense, a metaphorical, unsatisfiable "great white master" may have taken up residence in Ellison's black superego. If this is the case, Ellison's unique bid to escape the parochialism of racist America may have led him into one of racism's most pernicious traps, an overbearing self-doubt.

Though heroic in artistic intention, the Ellison resolution to this Afro-American intellectual agon is humanistically disturbing. Victimized people are not the material upon which claims for equality and humanity are secured. Only those individuals capable of turning the victimization into art can secure for a people their historical significance. Art endures. Politics is transitory. People only live and then die.[44]

Notes

Introduction

1. Harold Cruse, *The Crisis of the Negro Intellectual* (New York: William Morrow, 1967).

2. For descriptive purposes, we can divide the black urban riots of the 1960s into three distinct phases: (1) the early phase, which includes Harlem (1964) and Watts (1965); (2) the middle phase, which includes Newark (1967) and Detroit (1966); and (3) the third phase, which includes those riots that took place after the assassination of Martin Luther King, Jr. (Washington, D.C., 1968).

3. By civil rights intelligentsia I am referring to individuals like Bayard Rustin, Robert Weaver, Kenneth Clark, John Hope Franklin, Thurgood Marshall, J. Saunders Redding, Martin L. King, Sterling Tucker, Roy Wilkins, and Whitney Young as well as various other intellectuals affiliated with organizations involved in the civil rights movement.

4. In his poem "Harlem," Langston Hughes asked: "What happens to a dream deferred? / Does it dry up / like a raisin in the sun? . . . *Or does it explode?* (*Selected Poems of Langston Hughes* [New York: Random House, 1990], p. 268).

5. Figures in this wing include Amiri Baraka, Dan Watts and the circles around *Liberator* magazine, Hoyt Fuller and the circles around *Negro Digest/Black World*, Stokeley Carmichael, Julius Lester, H. Rap Brown, Mualana Karenga, and Nikki Giovanni.

6. Stokeley Carmichael left the United States for Guinea in western Africa. In the process he changed his name to Kwame Toure to honor Kwame Nkrumah of Ghana, a father of Pan-Africanism, and Seko Toure of Guinea, a leader who was staunch in his advocacy of freedom for his country from French colonial and neocolonial domination.

7. The black political science organization, the National Conference of Black Political Scientists (NCOBPS), was founded in March 1969. The NCOBPS is a separate organization from the American Political Science Association. Its annual meetings are not held in conjunction with the larger organization.

8. Surprisingly, to date, there is no comprehensive study of the history and status of black studies programs in American academia. Historian Nathan Huggins authored a brief and rather cursory report on black studies for the Ford Foundation. See Huggins, *Afro-American Studies: A Report to the Ford Foundation* (New York: Ford Foundation, 1985).

9. Cruse later expands this deeply flawed line of argument in *Plural but Equal* (New York: William Morrow, 1987).

10. For an insightful biography of Du Bois that treats him as a "black-man-

of-culture" activist, see Arnold Rampersad, *The Art and Imagination of W. E. B. Du Bois* (Cambridge, Mass.: Harvard University Press, 1976).

11. See Mildred I. Thompson, *Ida B. Wells-Barnett: An Exploratory Study of an American Black Woman, 1893–1930* (Brooklyn: Carlson Publications, 1990), or a collection of Wells-Barnett's writings titled *Selected Works of Ida B. Wells-Barnett*, ed. Trudier Harris (New York: Oxford University Press, 1991).

12. See Stephen R. Fox, *The Guardian of Boston: William Monroe Trotter* (New York: Atheneum, 1970).

13. See Genna Rae McNeil, *Groundwork: Charles Hamilton Houston and the Struggle for Civil Rights* (Philadelphia: University of Pennsylvania Press, 1983).

14. For an explanation of the theoretical orientations of the Clarks' research, see William E. Cross, Jr., *Shades of Black: Diversity in African-American Identity* (Philadelphia: Temple University Press, 1991). For a discussion of their roles as "expert witnesses" in the *Brown* decision, see Mark A. Chesler, Joseph Sanders, and Debra S. Kalmuss, *Social Science in Court: Mobilizing Experts in the School Desegregation Cases* (Madison: University of Wisconsin Press, 1988).

15. See Pauli Murray, *Song in a Weary Throat: An American Pilgrimage* (New York: Harper and Row, 1987).

16. Historian Jackie Goggins has authored the first comprehensive scholarly biography of Woodson. See her *Carter G. Woodson: A Life in Black History* (Baton Rouge: Louisiana State University Press, 1993).

17. Martin Kilson, "Black Power: Anatomy of a Paradox," *Harvard Journal of Negro Affairs* 2, no. 1 (1968): 34.

18. Imamu Amiri Baraka (LeRoi Jones), *Raise Race Rays Raze: Essays since 1965* (New York: Random House, 1971), p. 98. For a more comprehensive discussion of Baraka's adherence to black nationalism, see Jerry Watts, *Engagement and Estrangement: Politics and Amiri Baraka / LeRoi Jones* (forthcoming).

19. For a discussion and critique of the black aesthetic movement, see Houston A. Baker's *The Journey Back: Issues in Black Literature and Criticism* (Chicago: University of Chicago Press, 1980), chap. 5, and *Blues, Ideology, and Afro-American Literature: A Vernacular Theory* (Chicago: University of Chicago Press, 1984); Charles Johnson's *Being and Race: Black Writing since 1970* (Bloomington: Indiana University Press, 1988).

20. See the companion volume to this one, Watts's *Engagement and Estrangement*.

21. Some of these important works are Karl Mannheim's *Ideology and Utopia: An Introduction to the Sociology of Knowledge*, trans. Louis Wirth and Edward Shils (New York: Harcourt, Brace and World, 1936); Alvin Gouldner's *The Future of Intellectuals and the Rise of the New Class* (New York: Seabury Press, 1979); Pierre Bourdieu's *Homo Academicus*, trans. Peter Collier (Stanford: Stanford University

Press, 1988); Edward Shils's *The Intellectuals and the Powers and Other Essays* (Chicago: University of Chicago Press, 1972); Robert Merton's *The Sociology of Science: Theoretical and Empirical Investigations* (Chicago: University of Chicago Press, 1973); Lewis Coser's *Men of Ideas: A Sociologist's View* (New York: Free Press, 1965); Daniel Bell's *The Winding Passage: Essays and Sociological Journeys, 1960–1980* (New York: Basic Books, 1980); Norman Birnbaum's *The Radical Renewal: The Politics of Ideas in Modern America* (New York: Pantheon, 1988); Seymour Martin Lipset's *Political Man: The Social Bases of Politics* (Baltimore: Johns Hopkins University Press, 1981); Zygmunt Bauman's *Legislators and Interpreters* (Ithaca: Cornell University Press, 1987); Robert Nisbet's *Tradition and Revolt: Historical and Sociological Essays* (New York: Random House, 1968); and Raymond Aron's *The Opium of the Intellectuals* (New York: Doubleday, 1957).

22. The concept of social marginality is discussed and analyzed in detail in my forthcoming study *Victims Revolt: Afro-American Intellectuals and the Politics of Ethnic Ambivalence.*

23. For a discussion of expatriation and an earlier generation of black female opera singers, see Rosalyn M. Story, *And So I Sing: African-American Divas of Opera and Concert* (New York: Warner Books, 1990). Errol Hill's *Shakespeare in Sable: A History of Black Shakespearean Actors* (Amherst: University of Massachusetts Press, 1984) discusses the journey to the European stage for blacks like Ira Aldridge, who desired to act in Shakespearean plays.

24. A much more elaborate and nuanced discussion of the victim status is found in Jerry G. Watts, *Victims Revolt.*

25. Orlando Patterson, "The Moral Crisis of the Black American," *Public Interest* 32 (Summer 1973): 52.

26. The key texts in this area are Frantz Fanon, *Black Skin, White Masks*, trans. Charles Lam Markmann (New York: Grove Press, 1967), and *The Wretched of the Earth*, trans. Constance Farrington (New York: Grove Press, 1968); Albert Memmi, *The Colonizer and the Colonized* (Boston: Beacon Press, 1967); Jean-Paul Sartre, *Anti-Semite and Jew*, trans. George J. Becker (New York: Schocken Books, 1948); and Paulo Freire, *Pedagogy of the Oppressed*, trans. Myra Bergman Ramos (New York: Seabury Press, 1974).

27. Ever concerned about the impression of whites, Wright stated that he had made a mistake in writing *Uncle Tom's Children*. He wrote: "When the reviews of that book began to appear I realized that I had made a terrible mistake. I found that I had written a book which even bankers' daughters could read and weep over and feel good about. *I swore to myself that if I ever wrote another book, no one would weep over it; that it would be so hard and deep that they would have to face it without the consolation of tears*" (my italics) (Richard Wright, "How 'Bigger' Was Born," *Saturday Review of Literature*, June 1, 1940, pp. 4–5, 17–20).

28. James Baldwin's prominence as a victim status ideologue is discussed in Jerry Watts, *Victims Victorious: Afro-American Intellectuals Embrace the Victim Status* (forthcoming).

29. The idea of ethnic marginality is derived from Robert Park's notion of the "Marginal Man." I have updated the term to take into account drastic changes in the quality of acculturation for black Americans. For a journey through the historical uses of the term as well as its contemporary theoretical applicability, see Watts, *Victims Revolt*, chap. one.

30. For a discussion of Toomer and Gurdjieff, see Rudolph P. Byrd, *Jean Toomer's Years with Gurdjieff: Portrait of an Artist, 1923–1936* (Athens: University of Georgia Press, 1990). For a more extensive discussion of the impact of social and ethnic marginality on Jean Toomer, see Watts, *Victim's Revolt.*

31. For a short introduction to this unique Afro-American intellectual, see Cox's essays in *Race, Class, and the World System: The Sociology of Oliver C. Cox*, ed. Herbert Hunter and Sameer Y. Abraham (New York: Monthly Review Press, 1987). Also see the editors' excellent introduction.

32. Albert Murray, *The Hero and The Blues* (Columbia: University of Missouri Press, 1973), p. 38.

CHAPTER 1

1. Jacqueline Covo, *The Blinking Eye: Ralph Waldo Ellison and His American, French, German, and Italian Critics, 1952–1971* (Metuchen, N.J.: Scarecrow Press, 1974).

2. Ibid., p. 13.

3. Nathan Scott, "Black Literature," in *Harvard Guide to Contemporary American Writing*, ed. Daniel Hoffman (Cambridge, Mass.: Harvard University Press, 1979), p. 295.

4. Covo, *Blinking Eye*, pp. 25–34. Covo notes that black intellectuals were excluded from the poll.

5. Norman Mailer, "Evaluations—Quick and Expensive Comments on the Talent in the Room," in *Advertisements for Myself* (New York: G. P. Putnam's Sons, 1981), p. 432.

6. Ralph Ellison, *Shadow and Act* (New York: Random House, 1964).

7. During lunch following a spring 1984 speaking engagement at the University of California, Davis, novelist Paule Marshall informed the gathering that Ellison's *Shadow and Act* was the most powerful criticism of black writing and writers yet published.

8. Stanley Edgar Hyman, "Ralph Ellison in Our Time," *New Leader*, October 26, 1964; reprinted in *Ralph Ellison: A Collection of Critical Essays*, ed. John Hersey (Englewood Cliffs: Prentice Hall, 1974), p. 42.

9. Ralph Ellison, *Going to the Territory* (New York: Random House, 1986).

10. David Bradley, review of *Going to the Territory*, *Los Angeles Times*, August 8, 1986; reprinted, in part, on the back cover of the paperback edition of *Going to the Territory*.

11. Ellison, "Hidden Name and Complex Fate," in *Shadow and Act*, p. 146.

12. For discussion of Ellison's life, see John Wright's "Dedicated Dreamer, Consecrated Acts: Shadowing Ellison," *Carleton Miscellany* 18, no. 3 (Winter 1980); Robert G. O'Meally's *The Craft of Ralph Ellison* (Cambridge, Mass.: Harvard University Press, 1980); and Jervis Anderson's profile of Ellison, "Going to the Territory," *New Yorker*, November 22, 1976.

13. In an interview, "The Art of Fiction," in *Shadow and Act*, Ellison stated, "I had been hunting since I was eleven, but no one had broken down the process of wing-shooting for me and it was from reading Hemingway that I learned to lead a bird. When he describes something in print, believe him; . . . he's been there" (p. 168). O'Meally reported this "confession" as if it were fact. He wrote, "Luckily, by reading Hemingway's descriptions of leading a bird in flight, Ellison became an excellent hunter during those lean months in Dayton" (O'Meally, *Craft of Ralph Ellison*, p. 32).

14. Kimberly W. Benston, in "Ellison, Baraka, and the Faces of Tradition," *Boundary 2* 6, no. 2 (Winter 1978): 333–54, shows how Ellison conspicuously misreads in order to situate himself in a tradition. For an argument similar to Benston's concerning Ellison's willingness to invent "literary ancestors," see Robert O'Meally's "The Rules of Magic: Hemingway as Ellison's 'Ancestor,'" *Southern Review* 21, no. 3 (Summer 1985): 751–69.

15. Some critics believe that Ellison has gone too far in creating these personal identity stories. Donald Gibson has written, "It is embarrassing to read that his horizons were broadened because he knew a white boy who was interested in electronics, because his mother brought home recordings of operas and copies of such magazines as *Vanity Fair*. It is embarrassing not because of the value it places on things 'white' and not even because of its denial of the values implicit in black life and culture, but because it is not true. It is too simplistic and too obvious an attempt to assert his nonblackness." See Gibson's discussion of the politics of Ellison and Baldwin in *The Politics of Twentieth-Century Novelists*, ed. George A. Panichas (New York: Thomas Y. Crowell, 1974), p. 309.

16. The "interview" with Ellison conducted by Robert Stepto and Michael Harper and included in *Chant of Saints*, ed. Michael S. Harper and Robert B. Stepto (Urbana: University of Illinois Press, 1979), is one such interview. A short discussion of Ellison's rewriting of a spontaneous interview conducted by Stepto and Harper and the interviewers' willingness to participate in the charade is contained in Stepto's "Let's Call Your Mama and Other Lies About Michael S. Harper," *Callaloo* 13 (Fall 1990), pp. 803–4.

17. For individuals who realize their identities through the written word, distaste for interviews is not uncommon. Asked why so many writers did not like being interviewed, novelist John Barth responded, "No doubt because our business is the considered word, not the spontaneous. We care as much for the how as for the what gets said, in print." See John Barth, *The Friday Book* (New York: G. P. Putnam's Sons, 1984), p. 172.

18. For celebrations of Ellison, see Jervis Anderson, "Going to the Territory," and Richard Kostelanetz, "Ralph Ellison: Novelist as Brown Skinned Aristocrat," *Shenandoah: The Washington and Lee University Review*, Summer 1969. In fact, contrary to its title, there is very little that can actually be said to be critical in Hersey's *Ralph Ellison: A Collection of Critical Essays*.

19. See "A Ralph Ellison Festival," *Carleton Miscellany* 18, no. 3 (Winter 1980), and Harper and Stepto, *Chant of Saints*, particularly the unengaging interview with Ellison conducted by Stepto and Harper.

20. Kerry McSweeney, *Invisible Man: Race and Identity* (Boston: Twayne Publishers, 1988), p. 21.

21. O'Meally, *Craft of Ralph Ellison*. Hopefully the book will soon be reissued in paperback so as to obtain the broader audience that it merits. The Alan Nadel text, *Invisible Criticism: Ralph Ellison and the American Canon* (Iowa City: University of Iowa Press, 1988), is a study of the ways in which Ellison simultaneously utilizes and critiques his American literary forebears in *Invisible Man*. Mark Busby's *Ralph Ellison* (Boston: Twayne Publishers, 1991) offers numerous insights into Ellison's intellectual style.

Besides the works of O'Meally, Nadel, and McSweeney, other recent studies of Ellison include Susan Resneck Parr and Pancho Savery, eds., *Approaches to Teaching Ellison's Invisible Man* (New York: Modern Language Association of America, 1989); Robert O'Meally, ed., *New Essays on Invisible Man* (New York: Cambridge University Press, 1988); Michael Lynch, *Creative Revolt: A Study of Wright, Ellison, and Dostoevsky* (New York: Peter Lang, 1990); and Kimberly W. Benston, ed., *Speaking for You: The Vision of Ralph Ellison* (Washington, D.C.: Howard University Press, 1987).

22. See the special issue on Ellison in *Black World* (December 1970), particularly the essays by Ernest Kaiser and Clifford Mason. Kaiser is a throwback to an earlier generation of black leftists, Communist Party members, and fellow travelers who attacked *Invisible Man* upon its publication. Ellison has had the rare honor of being attacked by black leftists and black nationalists. Abner Berry, a black Communist Party member, reviewed *Invisible Man* for the Communist *Daily Worker* on June 1, 1952. He wrote: "Written in the vein of middle class snobbishness—even contempt—towards the Negro people, Ellison's work manipulates his nameless hero for 439 pages through a maze of corruption, brutality, anti-communism slanders, sex perversion and the sundry inhumani-

ties upon which a dying social system feeds. . . . There are no real characters in *Invisible Man*, nor are there any realistic situations. . . . In effect, it is 439 pages of contempt for humanity written in an affected, pretentious, and other worldly style to suit the kingpins of world white supremacy." In the June 1952 edition of Paul Robeson's *Freedom*, John Oliver Killens reviewed the book. He concluded that "the Negro people need Ralph Ellison's *Invisible Man* like we need a hole in the head or a stab in the back. . . . It is a vicious distortion of Negro Life" (p. 7).

23. Clifford Mason, "Ralph Ellison and the Underground Man," *Black World*, December 1970, p. 21.

24. O'Meally, *Craft of Ralph Ellison*, p. 179.

25. One of the few black writers to raise this point has been Nikki Giovanni. See her comments in *Black Women Writers (1950–1980): A Critical Evaluation*, ed. Mari Evans (Garden City: Anchor Press, 1984), p. 205.

26. In James Alan McPherson's essay "Indivisible Man," in Hersey's *Ralph Ellison*, Ellison responds to a query concerning his apprehensions about the quality of the new novel: "But you want to be sure when you write so slowly, because if it's not good, if it's just passable, they'll be terribly disappointed" (p. 56). It is sometimes forgotten that the writing of *Invisible Man* was a long and tortured process for Ellison. See Langston Hughes's comments on the young writer Ellison's painstaking efforts in Arnold Rampersad's *I Dream a World: The Life of Langston Hughes*, vol. 2, *1941–1967* (New York: Oxford University Press, 1988), pp. 117, 118, 187, 192.

27. Kostelanetz, "Ralph Ellison," p. 65.

28. Scott, "Black Literature," p. 311.

29. See the discussion of Ellison in Houston Baker's *Blues, Ideology, and Afro-American Literature: A Vernacular Theory* (Chicago: University of Chicago Press, 1984), pp. 172–99.

30. Ibid.; O'Meally, *Craft of Ralph Ellison*, chap. 8; John Wright, "Dedicated Dreamer."

31. O'Meally, *Craft of Ralph Ellison*, p. 7. For a discussion of Oklahoma as a frontier land of perceived possibility, see John Thompson's *Closing the Frontier: Radical Responses in Oklahoma, 1889–1923* (Norman: University of Oklahoma Press, 1986). Thompson, however, omits a serious discussion of blacks.

32. In an interview with Richard Stern that was subsequently published in *Shadow and Act* as "That Same Pain, That Same Pleasure," Ellison described the Oklahoma of his youth. "Thus it had no tradition of slavery and while it was segregated, relations between the races were more fluid and thus more human than in the old slave states" (p. 5). Ellison is wrong concerning slavery in Oklahoma. There were numerous slaves in Oklahoma, many of whom were owned by American Indians. For a discussion of slavery in the Oklahoma Territory, see Rudi Halliburton, *Red over Black: Black Slavery among the Cherokee Indians* (West-

port, Conn.: Greenwood Press, 1977); Arthur Tolson, *The Black Oklahomans, a History: 1541–1972* (New Orleans: Edwards, 1974); and Joel Williamson, *The Crucible of Race: Black-White Relations in the American South since Emancipation* (New York: Oxford University Press, 1984). For a discussion of black life in the territory after emancipation, see Tolson, *Black Oklahomans,* and Jimmie L. Franklin, *Journey toward Hope: A History of Blacks in Oklahoma* (Norman: University of Oklahoma Press, 1982).

33. For a comprehensive description of the riot, see Scott Ellsworth's *Death in a Promised Land: The Tulsa Race Riot of 1921* (Baton Rouge: Louisiana State University Press, 1982).

34. See the John Hope Franklin introduction to Ellsworth, *Death in a Promised Land,* for an understanding of how the black community of Tulsa restored its sense of self and security in the aftermath of the riot.

Concerning the riot's impact on the racial sensitivity of black residents of Oklahoma City, Ellison stated, "We were pushed off to that what seemed the least desirable side of the city ... and our system of justice was based upon Texas law, yet there was an optimism within the Negro community and a sense of possibility which, despite our awareness of limitation (dramatized so brutally in the Tulsa race riot of 1921), transcended all of this" ("Remembering Jimmy," in *Shadow and Act,* p. 242). Around the same time as the Tulsa riot a black man was lynched in Oklahoma City. See LeRoy H. Fischer, ed., *Oklahoma's Governors 1907–1929: Turbulent Politics* (Oklahoma City: Oklahoma Historical Society, 1981), p. 107.

35. O'Meally, *Craft of Ralph Ellison,* pp. 7–8.

36. Ibid.

37. See the interview with Ellison in Hersey's *Ralph Ellison,* p. 15.

38. Ellison, "Hidden Name and Complex Fate," pp. 145–66.

39. Ibid.

40. Ellison discusses Oklahoma City and jazz in two essays in *Shadow and Act,* "The Charlie Christian Story" and "Remembering Jimmy." Also see the discussion of Oklahoma City in Albert Murray's *Stomping the Blues* (New York: McGraw-Hill, 1976).

41. Albert Murray, *Stomping the Blues,* pp. 152, 154, 155.

42. Ellison, "Remembering Jimmy."

43. O'Meally, *Craft of Ralph Ellison,* p. 9.

44. This episode is discussed in Jervis Anderson's "Going to the Territory."

45. O'Meally, *Craft of Ralph Ellison,* pp. 9–10.

46. Ellison, "The World and the Jug," in *Shadow and Act,* p. 135.

47. Ibid., p. 122.

48. During the tenure of Governor Henry Murray (1931–35) the Oklahoma National Guard was sent to close an Oklahoma City park to blacks. This epi-

· sode is significant but not because it makes Oklahoma appear to be like southern states in its enforcement of Jim Crow. What is significant is that racial boundaries were still in a state of flux and/or black Oklahoma City residents were sufficiently undeferential to existent racial boundaries. In either case, this is a state of affairs quite different from the typical racial practices and beliefs in the South in 1931. See LeRoy H. Fischer, ed., *Oklahoma's Governors, 1929–1955: Depression to Prosperity* (Oklahoma City: Oklahoma Historical Society, 1983), p. 63.

49. See the discussion of Tuskegee and Ellison's days there in O'Meally, *Craft of Ralph Ellison*, pp. 9–25.

50. See Albert Murray's discussion of Sprague in *South to a Very Old Place* (New York: McGraw-Hill, 1971), chap. 4. Murray is an alumnus of Tuskegee.

51. O'Meally, *Craft of Ralph Ellison*, p. 24.

52. Ibid., p. 30.

53. Ibid.

54. Ibid.

55. Hughes and Ellison appeared to sustain a rather warm relationship until the publication of *Invisible Man* in 1952. At that point Ellison openly rejected the black Harlem intellectual/artistic circles of Hughes. Ellison had long thought that these circles were less than intellectually "serious." Hughes, sensing Ellison's rejection, increasingly became disenchanted with the socially arrogant and more artistically successful younger writer. Nevertheless, Hughes continued to publicly praise Ellison the writer. See Rampersad, *I Dream a World*, pp. 200–202.

56. Harper and Stepto, *Chant of Saints*, p. 454.

57. Ellison, "That Same Pain," p. 15.

58. Ellison now consistently claims that Wright had little, if any, significant influence on his artistic life. Furthermore, Ellison's claim that Wright was out of touch with Afro-American folklore has now been accepted by many students of Afro-American literature, particularly those (à la Robert Stepto) who celebrate Ellison. See Stepto's Ellisonian discussion of Wright, "I Thought I Knew These People: Richard Wright and the Afro-American Literary Tradition," in *Chant of Saints*, ed. Harper and Stepto, pp. 195–211. Stepto's analysis is forced and may speak more to his ignorance of the dynamics between black intellectuals and the black "masses" than Wright's.

59. See Harper and Stepto, *Chant of Saints*, pp. 454–55.

60. O'Meally, *Craft of Ralph Ellison*, p. 30.

61. Ibid., pp. 30–31.

62. Ibid., pp. 31–32.

63. Ibid., p. 32.

64. Ibid., and O'Meally, "Rules of Magic."

65. O'Meally, *Craft of Ralph Ellison*, p. 32.

66. See Allen Geller interview with Ellison in *The Black American Writer*, vol. 1, *Fiction*, ed. C. W. E. Bigsby (Baltimore: Penguin Books, 1969), p. 154.

67. O'Meally, *Craft of Ralph Ellison*, pp. 33–36.

68. Mark Naison, *Communists in Harlem during the Depression* (Urbana: University of Illinois Press, 1983), p. 75.

69. Harold Cruse, *The Crisis of the Negro Intellectual* (London: W. H. Allen, 1969), p. 187.

70. O'Meally, *Craft of Ralph Ellison*, p. 54.

71. Ellison has stated on numerous occasions that he did not come to Harlem only to gain exposure to Harlem but to broaden his experience. He claims to have attended events throughout New York City that other blacks were not attending in significant numbers.

72. See the discussion of Wright's intellectual development in Michel Fabre's *The Unfinished Quest of Richard Wright*, trans. Isabel Barzun (New York: William Morrow, 1973); Constance Webb's *Richard Wright* (New York: G. P. Putnam's Sons, 1968); and Richard Wright's *American Hunger* (New York: Harper and Row, 1977).

73. Langston Hughes and Claude McKay also rose through the aid of the Left.

74. Webb, *Richard Wright*, p. 408.

75. We should be careful not to understate the depth of Ellison's commitment to Marxist thought during the late 1930s. See Michel Fabre's essay on the young Ellison's political beliefs, "From *Native Son* to *Invisible Man*: Some Notes on Ralph Ellison's Evolution in the 1950s," in *Speaking for You: The Vision of Ralph Ellison*, ed. Kimberly W. Benston (Washington, D.C.: Howard University Press, 1987).

76. It is a consistent theme throughout Ellison's commentary on other black writers that blacks often draw race around themselves too tightly, as if by merely proclaiming the particularity of black oppression they have functioned properly as black artists. This point is continually stated throughout *Shadow and Act* (p. 137). Ellison argued that the Negro writer's concern for expressing black victimization often blinded him or her to the need to master the writer's craft.

77. Ellison, "Some Questions and Some Answers," in *Shadow and Act*, pp. 261–72.

78. Larry Neal, "Politics and Ritual: Ellison's Zoot Suit," *Black World*, December 1970, pp. 37–38 (original emphasis).

79. Naison, *Communists in Harlem*, p. 218.

80. O'Meally, *Craft of Ralph Ellison*, p. 38.

81. Ibid.

82. Marcus Klein, *After Alienation: American Novels in Mid-Century* (Chicago: University of Chicago Press, 1964), pp. 91–93.

83. Neal, "Ellison's Zoot Suit," pp. 39–40.

84. "A Very Stern Discipline," an interview with Ellison, *Harper's*, March 1967, p. 88 (reprinted in Ellison, *Going to the Territory*).

85. Ibid., and O'Meally, *Craft of Ralph Ellison*, chaps. 3, 4, 8.

86. "A Very Stern Discipline," in Ellison, *Going to the Territory*, p. 292.

87. Ibid.

88. See Ellison's testimony before a congressional committee, "Harlem's America," *New Leader*, September 26, 1966, pp. 22–35.

89. Kostelanetz, "Ralph Ellison," p. 73.

90. Ellison, "Art of Fiction."

91. Kostelanetz, "Ralph Ellison," p. 74.

92. Nowhere in his discussions of his college and precollege days does Ellison mention political activism as having been a significant part of his life.

93. In his biography of Hughes, Rampersad notes that Hughes actually became somewhat angry at the degree to which Ellison retreated from the Harlem literary scene following the publication of *Invisible Man*. Ellison's disrespectful views of Hughes as an intellectual and writer can be found in Rampersad, *I Dream a World*, pp. 200–202.

Rampersad's biographies of Hughes have significantly improved contemporary assessments of Hughes's work. However, Hughes will undoubtedly always be seen as a less serious intellectual and/or writer than Wright, Ellison, and Baldwin. One telltale sign of this devaluation of Hughes lies in the fact that no serious literary scholar attempts (to my knowledge) to make Ellison an artistic protégé of Hughes despite the fact that Hughes took the young Ellison "under his arm" before Ellison met Wright. In fact, Hughes introduced Ellison to Wright.

94. See, among other studies, James Gilbert's *Writers and Partisans: A History of Literary Radicalism in America* (New York: John Wiley and Sons, 1968); Christopher Lasch's *The New Radicalism in America, 1889–1963: The Intellectual as a Social Type* (New York: Alfred Knopf, 1965); William Barrett's *The Truants: Adventures among the Intellectuals* (Garden City: Doubleday, 1982); Richard Pells's *Radical Visions and American Dreams* (New York: Harper and Row, 1973); and Daniel Aaron's *Writers on the Left: Episodes in American Literary Communism* (New York: Harcourt, Brace and World, 1961).

95. Alvin Gouldner, *The Future of Intellectuals and the Rise of the New Class* (New York: Seabury Press, 1979), particularly thesis six.

96. At some point during the early 1950s, Ellison was a member of the executive committee of the American Committee for Cultural Freedom. See Sidney Hook, *Out of Step: An Unquiet Life in the Twentieth Century* (New York: Carroll and Graf, 1987), p. 421.

The American Committee for Cultural Freedom was a weakly linked affiliate of the Congress for Cultural Freedom, which was based in Europe. The latter organization has since become known as having had CIA connections, though at the time, this affiliation was not known by many of the congress's participating intellectuals (à la Richard Wright). For a more extensive discussion of the American Committee for Cultural Freedom, see Christopher Lasch, *The Agony of the American Left* (New York: Vintage, 1968), chap. 3; and William Phillips, *A Partisan View: Five Decades of the Literary Life* (New York: Stein and Day, 1983), chaps. 13 and 14.

97. Daniel Bell, *The Winding Passage: Essays and Sociological Journeys, 1960–1980* (New York: Basic Books, 1980); see chap. 6, "The Intelligentsia in American Society," p. 128.

98. Norman Podhoretz, *Making It* (New York: Random House, 1967); see chap. 4, "The Family Tree," p. 110.

99. O'Meally, *Craft of Ralph Ellison*, chaps, 3, 4, 8.

100. A most emphatic and overstated critique of the weaknesses of the Communist Party's position toward Afro-American culture is of course Cruse's *Crisis of the Negro Intellectual.*

101. Ellison discusses his early artistic discipline in "Hidden Name and Complex Fate," particularly pp. 154–55, 160.

For a general discussion of Afro-American intellectual traditions, see Cornel West's "The Dilemma of the Black Intellectual," *Cultural Critique*, Fall 1985. The essay is simultaneously very perceptive and severely flawed. In his inability to wrestle with the limitations of formal Afro-American intellectual traditions West endows black jazz singers and black preachers with the label "intellectuals." Perhaps some jazz vocalists and preachers are intellectuals, but most are merely performers. Worse, the criteria West employs to substantiate their status as intellectuals are performance criteria. Certainly, jazz vocalists and preachers are linked to traditions, but they are not for the most part linked to intellectual traditions.

CHAPTER 2

1. Albert Murray, *The Omni-Americans* (New York: Outerbridge and Dienstfrey, 1970), p. 167.

For a short but perceptive discussion of Murray, see "Chitlins at the Waldorf: The Work of Albert Murray," chapter 6 of Stanley Crouch's *Notes of a Hanging Judge: Essays and Reviews, 1979–1989* (New York: Oxford University Press, 1990). Murray may well be the most understudied major black intellectual figure in America.

2. Ralph Ellison, "Richard Wright's Blues," in *Shadow and Act* (New York: Random House, 1964), pp. 78–79, 94.

3. Albert Murray, *The Hero and the Blues* (Columbia: University of Missouri Press, 1973), pp. 36–37, 106–7.

4. Ralph Ellison, "When Does a Black Join the Middle Class?," *Los Angeles Times*, January 29, 1975.

5. See "The Essential Ellison," an interview with Ellison conducted by Ishmael Reed, Quincy Troupe, and Steve Cannon, *Y'Bird* 1, no. 1 (1978): 133.

6. Ibid.

7. Mark Poster, *Existential Marxism in Postwar France: From Sartre to Althusser* (Princeton: Princeton University Press, 1975), p. 91.

8. Ibid., pp. 91–92 (original emphasis).

9. Albert Murray, *The Hero and the Blues*, p. 39 (original emphasis).

10. In *Black Literature in White America* (New Jersey: Barnes and Noble, 1982) Berndt Ostendorf is one of the few students of Ellison who recognizes that Ellison may have consistently romanticized black folk culture. See pp. 126–36.

11. See Robert Bocock, *Hegemony* (New York: Tavistock, 1986), for a concise discussion of Gramsci's notion of hegemony.

12. Poster, *Existential Marxism*, p. 149. For an argument that states that Merleau-Ponty blatantly misrepresented Sartre's notion of freedom, see David Detmer, *Freedom as a Value: A Critique of the Ethical Theory of Jean-Paul Sartre* (La Salle, Ill.: Open Court, 1986). If Detmer is correct, the misunderstood Sartre is similar to the understood Ellison.

13. Ellison's acontextual conception of freedom is far more nuanced than Albert Murray's notion. In criticizing James Baldwin's depiction of Harlem, Murray wrote, "What Baldwin writes about is not really life in Harlem. He writes about the economic and social conditions in Harlem, the material *plight* of Harlem" (*The Omni-Americans*, p. 149).

During a question-and-answer period following a lecture at Wesleyan University in the fall of 1984, Murray was asked how he could continue to hold to his blues-ontology acontextual notion of freedom, given the increased anomie, despair, and drug abuse in black inner-city neighborhoods. Murray responded concerning drug abuse, "I can't help it if someone doesn't want to be free."

14. Albert Murray, *The Hero and the Blues*, p. 107.

15. Charles A. Valentine, *Culture and Poverty: Critique and Counter-Proposals* (Chicago: University of Chicago Press, 1968).

16. Ellison, "An American Dilemma: A Review," in *Shadow and Act*, pp. 303–17.

17. Ibid., p. 313.

18. Ibid., p. 315.

19. Ibid.

20. Ibid., p. 317.

21. Valentine, *Culture and Poverty*, chap. 2. Ellison has always had a keen eye for

detecting simplistic and pejorative presuppositions about black life in the works of "experts on the Negro." Witness the prophetic genius in Ellison's insights into the rise of Jewish neoconservative critiques of the race problem (e.g., Norman Podhoretz, Nathan Glazer, and *Commentary* magazine). Though Podhoretz's parochialism toward blacks was easy to detect, Ellison sees through the liberal charade of Nathan Glazer. See Ellison's "No Apologies," *Harper's,* July 4, 1967, pp. 8–20.

22. Abram Kardiner and Lionel Ovesey, *The Mark of Oppression: Explorations in the Personality of the American Negro* (Cleveland: World Publishing, 1951), p. 385.

23. Ellison, "The World and the Jug," in *Shadow and Act*, p. 123. Ellison had discovered a Foucaultian discourse concerning black Americans much like that which created, according to Edward Said, the Orient. See Said's *Orientalism* (New York: Pantheon Books, 1978), chap. 1.

24. Ellison attacks black parochialism in two interviews, "The Essential Ellison," pp. 126–59, and "Study and Experience," in *Chant of Saints*, ed. Michael S. Harper and Robert B. Stepto (Urbana: University of Illinois Press, 1979), pp. 451–69.

Ellison's comments appeared on the cover of James Alan McPherson's *Hue and Cry*, a collection of short stories published in 1969 during the height of the "Black Arts" movement. In celebration of the nonblack nationalist black, McPherson, Ellison wrote:

> With this collection of stories, McPherson promises to move right past those talented but misguided writers of Negro American cultural background who take being black as a privilege for being obscenely second-rate and who regard their social predicament as Negroes as exempting them from the necessity of mastering the craft and forms of fiction. Indeed, as he makes his "hue and cry" over the dead-ends, the confusions of value and failures of sympathy and insight of those who habit this fictional world, McPherson's stories are themselves a hue and cry against the dead, publicity-sustained writing which has come increasingly to stand for what is called "black writing."

25. Ellison's views on Africa are found in Harold Isaacs, *The New World of Negro Americans* (New York: Viking Press, 1963), pp. 258–67.

26. Anthropologist John Szwed misunderstands Ellison in this regard. Szwed seems to think that the only basis for an Afro-American claim to cultural agency lies in tracing Afro-American culture to African and other New World black cultural sources. Ellison claims Afro-Americans' cultural agency as creators and creatures of an American culture void of African "retentions." See Szwed's "An American Anthropological Dilemma: The Politics of Afro-American Culture," in *Reinventing Anthropology*, ed. Dell Hymes (New York: Pantheon Books, 1972), pp. 153–81.

27. Hiram Haydn, *Words and Faces* (New York: Harcourt Brace Jovanovich, 1974), pp. 184–85. The antagonism that confronted Ellison on many college campuses during this period was captured in part by James Alan McPherson in "Indivisible Man," in *Ralph Ellison: A Collection of Critical Essays*, ed. John Hersey (Englewood Cliffs: Prentice Hall, 1974), pp. 43–57. It is also discussed by William Walling in "Art and Protest: Ralph Ellison's *Invisible Man* Twenty Years After," *Phylon* 34 (June 1973).

CHAPTER 3

1. See Irving Howe's "Black Boys and Native Sons," in *Decline of the New* (New York: Horizon Press, 1970), and Ellison's "The World and the Jug," in *Shadow and Act* (New York: Random House, 1964).

2. See my discussion of Howe in *Politics and the Ideology of the Victim Status* (forthcoming).

3. "Black Boys and Native Sons" was originally published in *Dissent*, Autumn 1963. Howe also wrote a response to Ellison's response, which was published in the *New Leader*, February 3, 1964.

4. The original Ellison essays appeared in the *New Leader* on December 9, 1963, and February 3, 1964.

5. "Everybody's Protest Novel" and "Many Thousands Gone" have been reprinted in Baldwin's *Notes of A Native Son* (New York: Bantam Books, 1972).

6. Howe, "Black Boys and Native Sons," p. 168.

7. Baldwin, "Many Thousands Gone," p. 28.

8. Baldwin, "Everybody's Protest Novel," p. 17.

9. Baldwin, "Many Thousands Gone," pp. 32–33, 34.

10. We should remember that producing fear and guilt in whites was one of Wright's primary goals. See "How Bigger Was Born," which had originally appeared in the *Saturday Review of Literature*, June 1, 1940.

11. This episode is mentioned in Michel Fabre's *The Unfinished Quest of Richard Wright*, trans. Isabel Barzun (New York: William Morrow, 1973), pp. 362–63, and Chester Himes's *The Quality of Hurt* (New York: Doubleday, 1972), pp. 199–201.

12. Ellison, "The World and the Jug," p. 17.

13. Howe, "Black Boys and Native Sons," pp. 169–70.

14. For a discussion of pre-Wright black intellectual and artistic themes, see S. P. Fullinwider, *The Mind and Mood of Black America* (Homewood, Ill.: Dorsey Press, 1969), and Robert Bone, *The Negro Novel in America* (New Haven: Yale University Press, 1965).

15. Howe, "Black Boys and Native Sons," p. 176.

16. Ibid.

17. Ibid., p. 181.

18. Ibid., pp. 182–83.

19. Irving Howe, "A Reply to Ralph Ellison," *New Leader*, February 3, 1964.

20. Ellison, "The World and the Jug," pp. 138–39.

21. Ibid., p. 139.

22. Howe, "Black Boys and Native Sons," p. 168.

23. See Howe's discussion of his intellectual development as a leftist in *A Margin of Hope* (New York: Harcourt Brace Jovanovich, 1982).

24. The Frankfurt school philosopher Herbert Marcuse also assumed this about blacks. See his noncritical discussion of blacks in *One-Dimensional Man: Studies in the Ideology of Advanced Industrial Societies* (Boston: Beacon Press, 1964).

25. James Alan McPherson captures this in his "Indivisible Man," in *Ralph Ellison: A Collection of Critical Essays*, ed. John Hersey (Englewood Cliffs: Prentice Hall, 1974), p. 54.

26. See the discussion of culture in J. Q. Merquior's *The Veil and the Mask: Essays on Culture and Ideology* (London: Routledge and Kegan Paul, 1979).

27. See Dennis Wrong's "The Oversocialized Conception of Man in Modern Sociology," in his collection of essays *Skeptical Sociology* (New York: Columbia University Press, 1976).

28. Mark Naison claims that the Communist Party was a major force among blacks in Harlem during the 1930s. It may have been, but it never obtained a large following in Harlem compared with other black political and social activities. Of course the reasons for its failure were many. Ellison's is just one, but a crucial one.

29. The inability of Marxism and Marxists to capture the essence of black life (in writings or political appeals) is a theme that Ellison constantly articulates, for he views Marxism as the deterministic social-scientific theory. Deterministic theories are usually seen as incapable of incorporating ironies and contradictions.

30. Ellison "The World and the Jug," p. 111.

31. Ibid., pp. 111–12.

32. Ibid., pp. 107–8.

33. Indeed, Ellison's entire agenda rests on making the unique black individual the standard-bearer for the entire ethnic group, which allows him to perceive far more diversity in the treatment of black Americans in the South (in the early 1960s and before) than was actually there.

34. Ellison, in "The World and the Jug," quotes selectively from Howe's review of Wright's short-story collection, *Eight Men*. The entire review is published in Howe's collection of reviews, *Celebrations and Attacks: Thirty Years of Literary and Cultural Commentary* (New York: Harcourt Brace Jovanovich, 1979). The review is very critical of Wright's artistic merits.

35. Ellison's point is correct, but it is far less significant than he would have us believe. For instance, *Native Son* and *Black Boy* could be considered very important if one is attempting to assess their influences on intellectuals (in America) during the last half century. Nevertheless, they remain less than first-rate pieces of art.

36. Ellison, "The World and the Jug," p. 137.

37. Ellison, "Harlem Is Nowhere," in *Shadow and Act*, p. 297.

38. Ibid., p. 299.

39. Ellison, "The World and the Jug," p. 112.

40. Ellison makes this claim about freedom and slavery in *Chant of Saints*, ed. Michael S. Harper and Robert B. Stepto (Urbana: University of Illinois Press, 1979).

41. Ellison, "The World and the Jug," pp. 127–28.

42. See discussion of the functionalist analysis of culture in Merquior, *The Veil and the Mask*, chap. 2.

43. Ellison, "The World and the Jug," p. 119.

44. Ibid., p. 120.

45. Ibid., p. 119.

46. Ibid., p. 120.

47. Ellison, "Richard Wright's Blues," in *Shadow and Act*, particularly p. 93.

48. André Malraux, *The Voices of Silence*, trans. Stuart Gilbert (Princeton: Princeton University Press, 1978), p. 642.

49. In a 1961 interview, Ellison had stated:

You might say that I was much less a social determinist. But I suppose that basically it comes down to a difference in our concepts of the individual. I, for instance, found it disturbing that Bigger Thomas had none of the finer qualities of Richard Wright, none of the imagination, none of the sense of poetry, none of the gaiety. And I preferred Richard Wright to Bigger Thomas. Do you see? Which gets you in on the—directs you back to the difference between what Wright was himself and how he conceived of the individual; back to his conception of the quality of Negro humanity. (*Shadow and Act*, p. 16)

50. Richard Wright, "How Bigger Was Born."

51. Ellison, "The World and the Jug," p. 120.

52. See the comparison of Wright and Ellison in Berndt Ostendorf's *Black Literature in White America* (New Jersey: Barnes and Noble, 1982), chap. 5.

53. For an example of such unfamiliarity, see Robert B. Stepto, "I Thought I Knew These People: Richard Wright and the Afro-American Literary Tradition," in *Chant of Saints*, ed. Harper and Stepto.

54. One does not imagine Ellison at any point in his life writing *White Man, Listen!* or *Twelve Million Black Voices*.

55. Ellison, "The Art of Fiction," in *Shadow and Act*, p. 169 (emphasis added).

56. Ellison, "The World and the Jug," p. 141.

57. Ibid., p. 122.

58. Wright's *Black Boy* is also an excellent discussion of black life in the Deep South during the early decades of the twentieth century, though Ellison believes it to be dishonest. Charles Davis, the late Yale University professor, also comments on the distortions in *Black Boy* in "From Experience to Eloquence: Richard Wright's *Black Boy* as Art," in *Chant of Saints*, ed. Harper and Stepto. One again wonders if Ellison and the neo-Ellisonian Davis simply lost sight of the forest when analyzing particular trees missing from Wright's "autobiography."

59. Ellison, "The World and the Jug," p. 135.

60. Ellison, "What These Children Are Like," in *Going to the Territory* (New York: Random House, 1986), pp. 65, 70–71.

61. Horace R. Cayton, *Long Old Road* (Seattle: University of Washington Press, 1964), pp. 191–92, 194.

For a different, more positive view of Tuskegee, see Albert Murray's *South to a Very Old Place* (New York: McGraw-Hill, 1971). Murray, a former student at the institute, remembers it fondly as an intellectually stimulating environment. In some respects Murray's views of Tuskegee need not conflict with those of Cayton. Murray speaks to the presence of a marginal intellectual subculture at Tuskegee, which is perhaps the most that one might find at many American colleges and universities. After all, we have to accept the fact that in Murray and Ellison, Tuskegee helped to train two of twentieth-century America's most prominent men of letters.

62. Ellison, "The World and the Jug," p. 135.

63. See Jean E. Cazort and Constance Tibs Hobson, *Born To Play: The Life and Career of Hazel Harrison* (Westport, Conn.: Greenwood Press, 1983).

64. The dedication read, "For Morteza Sprague: A Dedicated Dreamer in a Land Most Strange."

65. Ellison, "The World and the Jug," p. 116.

66. See Wright's discussion of freedom in his *Twelve Million Black Voices* (New York: Arno Press, 1969); *Black Power: A Record of Reactions in a Land of Pathos* (New York: Harper and Row, 1954); and *White Man, Listen!* (New York: Doubleday, 1957).

67. Howe, "Reply to Ralph Ellison," p. 14.

68. Ellison treats race and ethnicity as if they are natural, ordered categories for individual membership and realization.

69. Ellison, "The Little Man at Chehaw Station," in *Going to the Territory*, pp. 3–38. The "little man" is represented by the black coal-heavers sitting before a blazing furnace in a sordid basement of a New York City tenement who are overheard by a young Ellison discussing the qualities of the voices of various

Metropolitan Opera divas. Stunned by this violation of his ordered sensibilities, Ellison inquires as to the origins of their knowledge of the opera and discovers that they are Met extras. In this apparent contradiction lies the "little man at Chehaw Station."

70. See Hannah Arendt's essay "The Jew as Pariah," in her collection *The Jew as Pariah*, ed. Ron H. Felman (New York: Grove Press, 1978), or David Riesman's "A Philosophy for Minority Living," in Riesman's *Individualism Reconsidered and Other Essays* (Glencoe, Ill.: Free Press, 1954), pp. 55–69.

71. Allison Davis, *Leadership, Love, and Aggression* (New York: Harcourt Brace Jovanovich, 1983), chap. 4.

72. See the discussion of Cayton's journey with Wright through the South in Horace Cayton's *Long Old Road*.

73. Howe, "Reply to Ralph Ellison," p. 13. In his 1982 autobiography, *A Margin of Hope* (New York: Harcourt Brace Jovanovich, 1982), Howe reflected on his debate with Ellison.

Some fifteen years later, engaged in a polemic about black writing with Ralph Ellison, I found myself cast, to my own surprise, in a Sartre-like position. I had written an essay on the fiction of Richard Wright, James Baldwin, and Ellison, stressing the dominance—indeed, the inescapability—of the "protest" theme in their work. Ellison objected that I had locked the black writers into an airless box—what Sartre would call their "situation." Ellison claimed for the blacks, as Rosenberg had for the Jews, an autonomous culture that could not be fully apprehended through the lens of "protest." Surely there was some validity to Ellison's argument, yet I could not help thinking that the "situation" of the blacks had generated more traumas, more scars than he was ready to admit. Perhaps, however, it was easier for me to see this with regard to blacks than Jews. Maybe there can be no clearcut resolution of such differences, first between Sartre and Rosenberg, and then between me and Ellison, since both sides overstress portions of recognizable truth. (p. 257)

74. Ellison, "The World and the Jug," p. 142.

75. Harold Cruse, *The Crisis of the Negro Intellectual* (London: W. H. Allen, 1969), pp. 507–8.

76. Ibid.

77. Albert Murray, *The Hero and the Blues* (Columbia: University of Missouri Press, 1973), p. 12.

78. Note the scathing book review of *Invisible Man* by John Oliver Killens in *Freedom*, June 1952. The review was so thoroughly dismissive of Ellison's talents that one can easily conclude that something more than an honest evaluation was at work in Killens's mind. Perhaps he had met his master and known not what to do.

79. In John Hersey's edited volume, *Ralph Ellison*, pp. 95–114.

80. Ibid., p. 110.

81. Ibid., pp. 110–11.

CHAPTER 4

1. Arnold Hauser, *The Sociology of Art*, trans. Kenneth Northcott (London: Routledge and Kegan Paul, 1982), pp. 567–68.

2. Ibid., p. 568.

3. Robert G. O'Meally, *The Craft of Ralph Ellison* (Cambridge, Mass.: Harvard University Press, 1980), p. 21.

4. Ibid., p. 2.

5. Ibid., pp. 2–3.

6. Ibid. Arnold Hauser, the Hungarian Marxist art historian vehemently disagreed with the Rourke-Ellison assertion. Writing in 1958, Hauser stated, "Folk art may be of immemorial antiquity, but the thesis that history begins with folk art, that all national literatures, for example, begin with a period of folk-poetry, has not been and cannot be proved." See Hauser, *The Philosophy of Art History* (Cleveland: World Publishing, 1963), pp. 308–9.

7. Gene Bluestein, *The Voice of the Folk* (Amherst: University of Massachusetts Press, 1972), p. 136.

8. Houston A. Baker, *Blues, Ideology, and Afro-American Literature: A Vernacular Theory* (Chicago: University of Chicago Press, 1984), p. 174.

Albert Murray would disagree with Ellison on this point. Murray wrote, "Both [Baldwin and Wright] profess great pride in Negroes, but in practice seem to rate the theories and abstract formulations of French existentialism over the infinitely richer wisdom of the blues. Both . . . seem to have missed what should be one of the most obvious implications of the blues tradition: *It is the product of the most complicated culture, and therefore the most complicated sensibility in the modern world*" (*The Omni-Americans* [New York: Outerbridge and Dienstfrey, 1970], p. 166 [original emphasis]).

9. Baker, *Blues, Ideology, and Afro-American Literature*, p. 174. The BBC program was recorded in May 1982 and was entitled "Garrulous Ghosts: The Literature of the American South."

10. Ibid., p. 175.

11. Hauser, *Sociology of Art*, p. 568.

12. Ibid., chap. 1, and Joan Shelley Rubin's *Constance Rourke and American Culture* (Chapel Hill: University of North Carolina Press, 1980). Also see J. Q. Merquior's discussion of Herder in Merquior, *The Veil and the Mask: Essays on Culture and Ideology* (London: Routledge and Kegan Paul, 1979).

13. Merquior, *The Veil and the Mask*, chap. 2, "Remarks on the Theory of Culture."

14. Ibid., p. 41.

15. Ibid.

16. Ibid.

17. Ibid., p. 43–44.

18. Ibid., pp. 53–61.

19. Ibid., p. 53 (emphasis added).

20. Ellison does not want people to think that a fine artist like himself, Baldwin, or even Wright rose spontaneously from black everyday life. Ellison has stated, "He [Wright] was as much a product of his reading as of his painful experiences, and he made himself a writer by subjecting himself to the writer's discipline—as he understood it. The same is true of James Baldwin, who is not the product of a Negro store-front church but of the library, and the same is true of me" (*Shadow and Act* [New York: Random House, 1964], p. 116).

21. It is for this reason that Harold Cruse misunderstands Ellison in *The Crisis of the Negro Intellectual* (London: W. H. Allen, 1969), pp. 505–11; Larry Neal also misreads Ellison in this manner in his "Politics and Ritual: Ellison's Zoot Suit," *Black World*, December 1970.

22. Ostendorf, *Black Literature in White America* (New Jersey: Barnes and Noble, 1982), pp. 126–28.

23. Popular culture versus mass culture versus folk culture is discussed by Hauser in *Sociology of Art* as well as by Herbert Gans in *Popular Culture and High Culture* (New York: Basic Books, 1974). My belief in the demise of most authentic American folk cultures, however, stems from my reading of Stuart Ewen's *Captains of Consciousness: Advertising and the Roots of Consumer Culture* (New York: McGraw-Hill, 1976) and his collaboration with his wife, Elizabeth Ewen, *Channels of Desire: Mass Images and the Shaping of American Consciousness* (New York: McGraw-Hill, 1982). I have also been influenced by my reading of Max Horkheimer and Theodor W. Adorno's *Dialectic of Enlightenment*, trans. John Cumming (New York: Herder and Herder, 1969), particularly chap. 4, "The Culture Industry: Enlightenment as Mass Deception."

24. Once again the Herdian romanticism of Ellison comes to light. Concerning such romanticism, Hauser has written, "Romanticism deprived folk-art of its concrete historical features and changed it instead into a conceptually imprecise phenomenon undefined as to its origins in order to emphasize its supposedly universal and prototypical nature" (*Sociology of Art*, p. 566).

25. Ellison, "What These Children Are Like," in *Going to the Territory* (New York: Random House, 1986), pp. 71–72 (emphasis added).

26. Ellison would view it as a typical irony of American culture that the same

Irish Catholics who cheer the black players on the Boston Red Sox would utter vile racist insults at black children attempting to integrate South Boston public schools. Yet, history has repeatedly shown that a cultural insider status does not preclude political exclusion. After all, Jews were Germans.

27. Geoffrey H. Hartman, *André Malraux* (New York: Hillary House, 1960), p. 91.

28. See Elijah Anderson, *Street Wise: Race, Class, and Change in an Urban Community* (Chicago: University of Chicago Press, 1990). For a reflective essay on black urban breakdown, see Cornel West, "Nihilism in Black America," *Dissent*, Spring 1991.

29. For an extensive discussion of slavery and black folklore, see Lawrence Levine, *Black Culture and Black Consciousness: Afro-American Folk Thought from Slavery to Freedom* (New York: Oxford University Press, 1977), chaps. 1 and 2.

30. James C. Scott's *Domination and the Arts of Resistance* (New Haven: Yale University Press, 1990) and his earlier work, *Weapons of the Weak: Everyday Forms of Peasant Resistance* (New Haven: Yale University Press, 1985), provide provocative insights into the ways that subjugated peoples maintain self-affirming oppositional discourses beneath their apparent deference to the superior power of an oppressor.

31. Orlando Patterson uses the term "natal alienation" to describe one of the key aspects of the social status of a slave, for slaves were denied rights to their forebears and their progeny. See Patterson's *Slavery and Social Death: A Comparative Study* (Cambridge, Mass.: Harvard University Press, 1982).

32. For an insightful discussion of one variety of intellectual heroic individualism, see Leslie Paul Thiele, *Friedrich Nietzsche and the Politics of the Soul: A Study of Heroic Individualism* (Princeton: Princeton University Press, 1990).

33. Miguel de Unamuno, *The Tragic Sense of Life in Men and Nations*, trans. Anthony Kerrigan (Princeton: Princeton University Press, 1972).

34. Victor Ouimette, *Reason Aflame: Unamuno and the Heroic Will* (New Haven: Yale University Press, 1974), p. 49. For a discussion of Unamuno's influence on Ellison, see John Wright's ambitious essay, "Dedicated Dreamer, Consecrated Acts: Shadowing Ellison," in a special issue of the *Carleton Miscellany* 18, no. 3 (Winter 1980). A shorter version of the Wright essay appears in *Speaking for You: The Vision of Ralph Ellison*, ed. Kimberly W. Benston (Washington, D.C.: Howard University Press, 1987).

35. Michael S. Harper and Robert B. Stepto, eds., *Chant of Saints* (Urbana: University of Illinois Press, 1979), pp. 461–62.

36. See Ellison's comments on black artists and the American Academy of Arts and Letters in "The Essential Ellison," an interview conducted by Ishmael Reed, Quincy Troupe, and Steve Cannon, *Y'Bird* 1, no. 1 (1978).

37. In an interview with James Baldwin that was originally published in the *Paris Review* during the spring of 1984, the following exchange took place:

BALDWIN: . . . As for Ralph [Ellison], I haven't seen him in many years.

INTERVIEWER: You haven't corresponded at all?

BALDWIN: No, I gather Ralph did not like what he considered I was doing on the civil rights road. And so, we haven't seen each other. (See Fred L. Standley and Louis H. Pratt, eds., *Conversations with James Baldwin* [Jackson: University Press of Mississippi, 1989], p. 252.)

Perhaps Baldwin had read the interview with Ellison in which the author of *Invisible Man* questions the rationality of Baldwin's willingness to function as a spokesperson for the civil rights movement. See the Allen Geller interview in the *Tamarack Review*, October 1963, reprinted in *The Black American Writer*, vol. 1, *Fiction*, ed. C. W. E. Bigsby (Baltimore: Penguin Books, 1969), pp. 153–68.

38. See the Joe Walker interview with Baldwin in *Conversations with James Baldwin*, ed. Stanley and Pratt, p. 132.

39. Ellison, *Shadow and Act*, p. 137.

40. My personal experience is quite the opposite of Ellison's depiction. Between 1984 and 1990 I was a faculty member at Wesleyan University in Middletown, Connecticut. With a reputation for liberalism, Wesleyan had developed a rather well known program in ethnomusicology and world music. However, the music of black people, whether Afro-American or African, was thoroughly devalued within this program and the university administration. Ed Blackwell, one of the premier craftsman in American music, was treated in what could only be considered an extraordinarily racist fashion. Instead of being a standardbearer of the program, a position he meritocratically deserved, he was treated like a third-rate appendage. Other less well known but talented black jazz musicians (à la Bill Lowe) were treated in an equally sick manner. Interestingly, it became clear that the university felt that it could mistreat jazz musicians because they really did not have many other options for steady teaching incomes. I am reminded of what a chair of the English department once said. When told that a colleague was going to listen to a practice session of a jazz combo, the professor uttered, "Oh, do they practice"?

In 1965 the trustees of Columbia University overruled an advisory board that had unanimously recommended Duke Ellington for a Pulitzer Prize for longterm achievement. In 1970 Ellington was elected to the American Academy and Institute of Arts and Letters, the only jazz composer ever so honored. See Cruse, *Crisis of the Negro Intellectual*, pp. 107–11.

For a discussion of the continual refusal of the American Academy and Institute of Arts and Letters to treat jazz as a serious art form, see Gary Giddins's "What American Academy?," *Village Voice*, June 23, 1992. Whence comes Ellison's claim?

41. See the discussion on black writers and the publishing industry in "The Negro in American Culture," a roundtable discussion featuring James Baldwin, Langston Hughes, Lorraine Hansberry, Nat Hentoff, Alfred Kazin, and Emile Capouya, in *Black American Writer*, ed. Bigsby, pp. 79–108. In the same volume, see Hughes, "The Problems of the Negro Writer: The Bread and Butter Side," pp. 65–67, and John A. Williams, "The Problems of the Negro Writer: The Literary Ghetto," pp. 67–69.

42. In the interview with Allen Geller published in the *Tamarack Review*, October 1963, Ellison is asked, "What role are you playing politically?" Ellison states, "What do I do? I belong to the Committee of One Hundred which is an arm of the legal defense committee of the NAACP. I vote. I try to vote responsibly. I contribute whenever I can to efforts to improve things. Right now one of the things I'm trying to do is to point out that it's a more complex problem than that of simply thrusting out your chin and saying 'I'm defiant.'"

43. Concerning Ellison's elitist self-definition, Norman Podhoretz once wrote,

> For my part I found Ellison the man stuffy and pompous; he was in truth amazingly like one of the characters he himself had satirized for those very qualities in *Invisible Man*. He also struck me as a Negro equivalent of certain prissy German Jews I knew (*yeckes*, in the derogatory Yiddish term for the type) who were forever preening themselves on their superior refinement, education and culture. Once I even heard him declare in a statement that could easily have issued from the lips of a typical *yecke* but was, as with so much about Ellison's personality, very hard to square with the author of *Invisible Man*: "As for me, I have values." (*Breaking Ranks: A Political Memoir* [New York: Harper and Row, 1979], p. 133)

44. In "The World and the Jug," Ellison makes the following revealing comment: "I also know of another really quite brilliant writer who, under the advice of certain wise men who were then managing the consciences of artists, abandoned the prison of his writing to go to Spain, where he was allowed to throw away his life defending a worthless hill. I have not heard his name in years but I remember it vividly: it was Christopher Cauldwell, né Christopher St. John Sprigg." Ellison would have us believe that a man who chose to fight against the spread of fascism in Spain threw his life away defending a worthless hill. In some respects, Ellison's disrespect and trivialization of those who have actually struggled against tyranny as opposed to those, like himself, who merely write about the human desire for freedom is myopic, selfish, and thoroughly disgust-

ing. One may wonder what Ellison thinks about those black Americans who lost their lives on "worthless hills" struggling against white supremacy. See *Shadow and Act*, p. 142.

It is very important to note that Ellison's understanding of the heroic always leads to individualization. Heroism done without a desire for individual recognition is, in Ellison's eyes, a heroism wasted. Ironically, those who struggle amidst anonymity are perhaps the most heroic figures.

Aaron, Daniel. *Writers on the Left: Episodes in American Literary Communism*. New York: Harcourt, Brace and World, 1961.

Anderson, Elijah. *Street Wise: Race, Class, and Change in an Urban Community*. Chicago: University of Chicago Press, 1990.

Anderson, Jervis. "Going to the Territory." *New Yorker*, November 22, 1976.

Arendt, Hannah. *The Jew as Pariah*. Edited by Ron H. Felman. New York: Grove Press, 1978.

Baker, Houston A. *Blues, Ideology, and Afro-American Literature: A Vernacular Theory*. Chicago: University of Chicago Press, 1984.

———. *The Journey Back: Issues in Black Literature and Criticism*. Chicago: University of Chicago Press, 1980.

Baldwin, James. *Notes of a Native Son*. New York: Bantam Books, 1972.

Baraka, Imamu Amiri [LeRoi Jones]. *Raise Race Rays Raze: Essays since 1965*. New York: Random House, 1971.

Barrett, William. *The Truants: Adventures among the Intellectuals*. Garden City: Doubleday, 1982.

Barth, John. *The Friday Book*. New York: G. P. Putnam's Sons, 1984.

Bell, Daniel. *The Winding Passage: Essays and Sociological Journeys, 1960–1980*. New York: Basic Books, 1980.

Benston, Kimberly W. "Ellison, Baraka, and the Faces of Tradition." *Boundary 2* 6, no. 2 (Winter 1978).

———, ed. *Speaking for You: The Vision of Ralph Ellison*. Washington, D.C.: Howard University Press, 1987.

Berube, Michael. *Marginal Forces / Cultural Centers: Tolson, Pynchon, and the Politics of the Canon*. Ithaca: Cornell University Press, 1992.

Bigsby, C. W. E., ed. *The Black American Writer*. Vol. 1, *Fiction*. Baltimore: Penguin Books, 1969.

Black World, December 1970. Special issue on Ralph Ellison.

Blanchot, Maurice. *The Space of Literature*. Translated by Ann Smock. Lincoln: University of Nebraska Press, 1983.

Blend, Charles D. *André Malraux: Tragic Humanist*. Columbus: Ohio State University Press, 1963.

Bluestein, Gene. *The Voice of the Folk*. Amherst: University of Massachusetts Press, 1972.

Bocock, Robert. *Hegemony*. New York: Tavistock, 1986.

Bone, Robert. *The Negro Novel in America*. New Haven: Yale University Press, 1972.

Busby, Mark. *Ralph Ellison*. Boston: Twayne Publishers, 1991.

Byrd, Rudolph P. *Jean Toomer's Years with Gurdjieff: Portrait of an Artist, 1923–1936*. Athens: University of Georgia Press, 1990.

Cayton, Horace R. *Long Old Road*. Seattle: University of Washington Press, 1964.

Cazort, Jean E., and Constance Tibs Hobson. *Born to Play: The Life and Career of Hazel Harrison*. Westport, Conn.: Greenwood Press, 1983.

Chesler, Mark A., Joseph Sanders, and Debra S. Kalmuss. *Social Science in Court: Mobilizing Experts in the School Desegregation Cases*. Madison: University of Wisconsin Press, 1988.

Covo, Jacqueline. *The Blinking Eye: Ralph Waldo Ellison and His American, French, German, and Italian Critics, 1952–1971*. Metuchen, N.J.: Scarecrow Press, 1974.

Cross, William E., Jr. *Shades of Black: Diversity in African-American Identity*. Philadelphia: Temple University Press, 1991.

Crouch, Stanley. *Notes of a Hanging Judge: Essays and Reviews, 1979–1989*. New York: Oxford University Press, 1990.

Cruse, Harold. *The Crisis of the Negro Intellectual*. New York: William Morrow, 1967.

——. *Plural but Equal*. New York: William Morrow, 1987.

Davis, Allison. *Leadership, Love, and Aggression*. New York: Harcourt Brace Jovanovich, 1983.

Detmer, David. *Freedom as a Value: A Critique of the Ethical Theory of Jean-Paul Sartre*. LaSalle, Ill.: Open Court, 1986.

Ellison, Ralph. Book-jacket comment in *Hue and Cry*, by James A. McPherson. Boston: Atlantic Monthly Press, 1969.

——. "The Essential Ellison." Interview by Ishmael Reed, Quincy Troupe, and Steve Cannon. *Y'Bird* 1, no. 1 (1978).

——. *Going to the Territory*. New York: Random House, 1986.

——. "Harlem's America." *New Leader*, September 26, 1966.

——. *Invisible Man*. New York: Random House, 1952.

——. "No Apologies." *Harper's*, July 4, 1967.

——: *Shadow and Act*. New York: Random House, 1964.

——. "When Does a Black Join the Middle Class?" *Los Angeles Times*, January 29, 1975.

Ellsworth, Scott. *Death in a Promised Land: The Tulsa Race Riot of 1921*. Baton Rouge: Louisiana State University Press, 1982.

Evans, Mari, ed. *Black Women Writers (1950–1980): A Critical Evaluation*. Garden City: Anchor Press, 1984.

Ewen, Stuart. *Captains of Consciousness: Advertising and the Roots of Consumer Culture*. New York: McGraw-Hill, 1976.

Ewen, Stuart, and Elizabeth Ewen. *Channels of Desire: Mass Images and the Shaping of American Consciousness.* New York: McGraw-Hill, 1982.

Fabre, Michel. "From *Native Son* to *Invisible Man*: Some Notes on Ralph Ellison's Evolution in the 1950s." In *Speaking for You: The Vision of Ralph Ellison,* edited by Kimberly W. Benston, pp. 199–216. Washington, D.C.: Howard University Press, 1987.

———. *The Unfinished Quest of Richard Wright.* Translated by Isabel Barzun. New York: William Morrow, 1973.

Fanon, Frantz. *Black Skin, White Masks.* Translated by Charles Lam Markmann. New York: Grove Press, 1967.

———. *The Wretched of the Earth.* Translated by Constance Farrington. New York: Grove Press, 1968.

Farnsworth, Robert M. *Melvin Tolson, 1898–1966: Plain Talk and Poetic Prophecy.* Columbia: University of Missouri Press, 1984.

Fischer, LeRoy H., ed. *Oklahoma's Governors, 1907–1929: Turbulent Politics.* Oklahoma City: Oklahoma Historical Society, 1981.

———. *Oklahoma's Governors, 1929–1955: Depression to Prosperity.* Oklahoma City: Oklahoma Historical Society, 1983.

Fox, Stephen R. *The Guardian of Boston: William Monroe Trotter.* New York: Atheneum, 1970.

Franklin, Jimmie L. *Journey toward Hope: A History of Blacks in Oklahoma.* Norman: University of Oklahoma Press, 1982.

Frohock, W. M. *André Malraux and the Tragic Imagination.* Stanford: Stanford University Press, 1952.

Fullinwider, S. P. *The Mind and Mood of Black America.* Homewood, Ill.: Dorsey Press, 1969.

Gannon, Edward. *The Honor of Being a Man: The World of André Malraux.* Chicago: Loyola University Press, 1957.

Gans, Herbert. *Popular Culture and High Culture.* New York: Basic Books, 1974.

Gates, Henry Louis. *Figures in Black: Words, Signs, and the "Racial" Self.* New York: Oxford University Press, 1987.

Gayle, Addison, ed. *The Black Aesthetic.* New York: Doubleday, 1971.

———. *The Way of the New World: The Black Novel in America.* Garden City: Anchor Press, 1976.

Geller, Allen. "An Interview with Ralph Ellison." *Tamarack Review,* October 1963.

Giddins, Gary. "What American Academy?" *Village Voice,* June 23, 1992.

Gilbert, James. *Writers and Partisans: A History of Literary Radicalism in America.* New York: John Wiley and Sons, 1968.

Goldberger, Avriel. *Visions of a New Hero: The Heroic Life According to André*

Malraux and Earlier Advocates of Human Grandeur. Paris: M. J. Minard Lettres Modernes, 1965.

Gouldner, Alvin. *The Future of Intellectuals and the Rise of the New Class*. New York: Seabury Press, 1979.

Greenlee, James W. *Malraux's Heroes and History*. Dekalb: Northern Illinois University Press, 1975.

Halliburton, Rudi. *Red over Black: Black Slavery among the Cherokee Indians*. Westport, Conn.: Greenwood Press, 1977.

Harper, Michael S., and Robert B. Stepto, eds. *Chant of Saints*. Urbana: University of Illinois Press, 1979.

Hartman, Geoffrey H. *André Malraux*. New York: Hillary House, 1960.

Hauser, Arnold. *The Philosophy of Art History*. Cleveland: World Publishing, 1963.

———. *The Sociology of Art*. Translated by Kenneth Northcott. London: Routledge and Kegan Paul, 1982.

Haydn, Hiram. *Words and Faces*. New York: Harcourt Brace Jovanovich, 1974.

Haywood, Harry. *Negro Liberation*. 1948. Reprint, Chicago: Liberator Press, 1976.

Hersey, John, ed. *Ralph Ellison: A Collection of Critical Essays*. Englewood Cliffs: Prentice Hall, 1974.

Himes, Chester. *The Quality of Hurt*. New York: Doubleday, 1972.

Hoffman, Daniel, ed. *Harvard Guide to Contemporary American Writing*. Cambridge, Mass.: Harvard University Press, 1979.

Hook, Sidney. *Out of Step: An Unquiet Life in the Twentieth Century*. New York: Carroll and Graf, 1987.

Horkheimer, Max, and Theodor W. Adorno. *Dialectic of Enlightenment*. Translated by John Cumming. New York: Herder and Herder, 1969.

Howe, Irving. *Celebrations and Attacks: Thirty Years of Literary and Cultural Commentary*. New York: Harcourt Brace Jovanovich, 1979.

———. *Decline of the New*. New York: Horizon Press, 1970.

———. *A Margin of Hope*. New York: Harcourt Brace Jovanovich, 1982.

Huggins, Nathan. *Afro-American Studies: A Report to the Ford Foundation*. New York: Ford Foundation, 1985.

Hunter, Herbert, and Sameer Y. Abraham, eds. *Race, Class, and the World System: The Sociology of Oliver C. Cox*. New York: Monthly Review Press, 1987.

Hyman, Stanley Edgar. "Ralph Ellison in Our Time." *New Leader*, October 26, 1964.

Hymes, Dell, ed. *Reinventing Anthropology*. New York: Pantheon Books, 1972.

Isaacs, Harold. *The New World of Negro Americans*. New York: Viking Press, 1963.

Jenkins, Cecil. *André Malraux*. New York: Twayne Publishers, 1972.

Johnson, Charles. *Being and Race: Black Writing since 1970*. Bloomington: Indiana University Press, 1988.

Kardiner, Abram, and Lionel Ovesey. *The Mark of Oppression: Explorations in the Personality of the American Negro*. Cleveland: World Publishing, 1951.

Kilson, Martin. "Black Power: Anatomy of a Paradox." *Harvard Journal of Negro Affairs* 2, no. 1 (1968).

Klein, Marcus. *After Alienation: American Novels in Mid-Century*. Chicago: University of Chicago Press, 1964.

Kluger, Richard. *Simple Justice: The History of Brown v. Board of Education and Black America's Struggle for Equality*. New York: Alfred Knopf, 1976.

Kostelanetz, Richard. *Politics in the Afro-American Novel*. New York: Greenwood Press, 1991.

——. "Ralph Ellison: Novelist as Brown Skinned Aristocrat." *Shenandoah: The Washington and Lee University Review*, Summer 1969.

Lasch, Christopher. *The Agony of the American Left*. New York: Vintage, 1968.

——. *The New Radicalism in America, 1889–1963: The Intellectual as a Social Type*. New York: Alfred Knopf, 1965.

Levine, Lawrence. *Black Culture and Black Consciousness: Afro-American Folk Thought from Slavery to Freedom*. New York: Oxford University Press, 1977.

Lynch, Michael. *Creative Revolt: A Study of Wright, Ellison, and Dostoevsky*. New York: Peter Lang, 1990.

McNeil, Genna Rae. *Groundwork: Charles Hamilton Houston and the Struggle for Civil Rights*. Philadelphia: University of Pennsylvania Press, 1983.

McSweeney, Kerry. *Invisible Man: Race and Identity*. Boston: Twayne Publishers, 1988.

Mailer, Norman. *Advertisements for Myself*. New York: G. P. Putnam's Sons, 1981.

Malraux, André. *The Metamorphosis of the Gods*. Translated by Stuart Gilbert. Garden City: Doubleday, 1960.

——. *The Psychology of Art*. Vol. 1, *Museum without Walls*. Translated by Stuart Gilbert. New York: Pantheon Books, 1949.

——. *The Psychology of Art*. Vol. 2, *The Creative Act*. Translated by Stuart Gilbert. New York: Pantheon Books, 1949.

——. *The Psychology of Art*. Vol. 3, *The Twilight of the Absolute*. Translated by Stuart Gilbert. New York: Pantheon Books, 1950.

——. *The Voices of Silence*. Translated by Stuart Gilbert. Princeton: Princeton University Press, 1978.

Marcuse, Herbert. *One-Dimensional Man: Studies in the Ideology of Advanced Industrial Societies*. Boston: Beacon Press, 1964.

Mason, Clifford. "Ralph Ellison and the Underground Man." *Black World*, December 1970.

Merquior, J. Q. *The Veil and the Mask: Essays on Culture and Ideology*. London: Routledge and Kegan Paul, 1979.

Murray, Albert. *The Hero and the Blues*. Columbia: University of Missouri Press, 1973.

———. *The Omni-Americans*. New York: Outerbridge and Dienstfrey, 1970.

———. *South to a Very Old Place*. New York: McGraw-Hill, 1971.

———. *Stomping the Blues*. New York: McGraw-Hill, 1976.

Murray, Pauli. *Song in a Weary Throat: An American Pilgrimage*. New York: Harper and Row, 1987.

Nadel, Alan. *Invisible Criticism: Ralph Ellison and the American Canon*. Iowa City: University of Iowa Press, 1988.

Naison, Mark. *Communists in Harlem during the Depression*. Urbana: University of Illinois Press, 1983.

Neal, Larry. "Politics and Ritual: Ellison's Zoot Suit." *Black World*, December 1970.

O'Meally, Robert. *The Craft of Ralph Ellison*. Cambridge, Mass.: Harvard University Press, 1980.

———. "The Rules of Magic: Hemingway as Ellison's 'Ancestor.'" *Southern Review* 21, no. 3 (Summer 1985).

———, ed. *New Essays on Invisible Man*. New York: Cambridge University Press, 1988.

Ostendorf, Berndt. *Black Literature in White America*. New Jersey: Barnes and Noble, 1982.

Ouimette, Victor. *Reason Aflame: Unamuno and the Heroic Will*. New Haven: Yale University Press, 1974.

Panichas, George A. *The Politics of Twentieth-Century Novelists*. New York: Thomas Y. Crowell, 1974.

Parr, Susan Resneck, and Pancho Savery, eds. *Approaches to Teaching Ellison's Invisible Man*. New York: Modern Language Association of America, 1989.

Patterson, Orlando. "The Moral Crisis of the Black American." *Public Interest* 32 (Summer 1973).

———. *Slavery and Social Death: A Comparative Study*. Cambridge, Mass.: Harvard University Press, 1982.

Pells, Richard. *Radical Visions and American Dreams*. New York: Harper and Row, 1973.

Phillips, William. *A Partisan View: Five Decades of the Literary Life*. New York: Stein and Day, 1983.

Podhoretz, Norman. *Breaking Ranks: A Political Memoir*. New York: Harper and Row, 1979.

———. *Making It*. New York: Random House, 1967.

Poster, Mark. *Existential Marxism in Postwar France: From Sartre to Althusser.*
Princeton: Princeton University Press, 1975.

"A Ralph Ellison Festival." Special issue on Ralph Ellison. *Carleton Miscellany*
18, no. 3 (Winter 1980).

Rampersad, Arnold. *The Art and Imagination of W. E. B. Du Bois.* Cambridge,
Mass.: Harvard University Press, 1976.

———. *I Dream a World: The Life of Langston Hughes.* Vol. 2, *1941–1967.* New York:
Oxford University Press, 1988.

Riesman, David. *Individualism Reconsidered and Other Essays.* Glencoe, Ill.: Free
Press, 1954.

Roberts, John W. *From Trickster to Badman: The Black Folk Hero in Slavery and
Freedom.* Philadelphia: University of Pennsylvania Press, 1989.

Rubin, Joan Shelley. *Constance Rourke and American Culture.* Chapel Hill: University
of North Carolina Press, 1980.

Scott, James C. *Domination and the Arts of Resistance.* New Haven: Yale University
Press, 1990.

———. *Weapons of the Weak: Everyday Forms of Peasant Resistance.* New Haven: Yale
University Press, 1985.

Scott, Nathan. "Black Literature." In *Harvard Guide to Contemporary American
Writing,* edited by Daniel Hoffman, pp. 287–341. Cambridge, Mass.: Harvard University Press, 1979.

Smith, Bernard. *The Death of the Artist as Hero: Essays in History and Culture.*
Melbourne: Oxford University Press, 1988.

Standley, Fred L., and Louis H. Pratt, eds. *Conversations with James Baldwin.* Jackson: University Press of Mississippi, 1989.

Stepto, Robert. "I Thought I Knew These People: Richard Wright and the
Afro-American Literary Tradition." In *Chant of Saints,* edited by Michael S.
Harper and Robert B. Stepto, pp. 195–211. Urbana: University of Illinois
Press, 1979.

———. "Let's Call Your Mama and Other Lies about Michael S. Harper." *Callaloo* 13 (Fall 1990).

Sweeney, Kerry. *Invisible Man: Race and Identity.* Boston: Twayne Publishers,
1988.

Szwed, John. "An American Anthropological Dilemma: The Politics of Afro-American Culture." In *Reinventing Anthropology,* edited by Dell Hymes, pp.
153–81. New York: Pantheon Books, 1972.

Tannery, Claude. *Malraux, the Absolute Agnostic; or Metamorphosis as Universal
Law.* Translated by Teresa Lavender Fagan. Chicago: University of Chicago,
1991.

Thiele, Leslie Paul. *Friedrich Nietzsche and the Politics of the Soul: A Study of Heroic
Individualism.* Princeton: Princeton University Press, 1990.

Thompson, John. *Closing the Frontier: Radical Responses in Oklahoma, 1889–1923.* Norman: University of Oklahoma Press, 1986.

Thompson, Mildred I. *Ida B. Wells-Barnett: An Exploratory Study of an American Black Woman, 1893–1930.* Brooklyn: Carlson Publications, 1990.

Tolson, Arthur. *The Black Oklahomans, a History: 1541–1972.* New Orleans: Edwards, 1974.

Unamuno, Miguel de. *The Tragic Sense of Life in Men and Nations.* Translated by Anthony Kerrigan. Princeton: Princeton University Press, 1972.

Urgo, Joseph. *Novel Frames: Literature as Guide to Race, Sex, and History in American Culture.* Jackson: University Press of Mississippi, 1991.

Valentine, Charles A. *Culture and Poverty: Critique and Counter-Proposals.* Chicago: University of Chicago Press, 1968.

Walling, William. " 'Art' and 'Protest': Ralph Ellison's *Invisible Man* Twenty Years After." *Phylon* 34 (June 1973).

Webb, Constance. *Richard Wright.* New York: G. P. Putnam's Sons, 1968.

West, Cornel. "The Dilemma of the Black Intellectual." *Cultural Critique*, Fall 1985.

———. "Nihilism in Black America." *Dissent*, Spring 1991.

Wilkinson, David. *Malraux: An Essay in Political Criticism.* Cambridge, Mass.: Harvard University Press, 1967.

Williamson, Joel. *The Crucible of Race: Black-White Relations in the American South since Emancipation.* New York: Oxford University Press, 1984.

Wright, John. "Dedicated Dreamer, Consecrated Acts: Shadowing Ellison." *Carleton Miscellany* 18, no. 3 (Winter 1980).

Wright, Richard. *American Hunger.* New York: Harper and Row, 1977.

———. *Black Boy.* New York: Harper and Row, 1937.

———. *Black Power: A Record of Reactions in a Land of Pathos.* New York: Harper and Row, 1954.

———. "How Bigger Was Born." *Saturday Review of Literature*, June 1, 1940.

———. *Twelve Million Black Voices.* New York: Arno Press, 1969.

———. *White Man, Listen!* New York: Doubleday, 1957.

Wrong, Dennis. *Skeptical Sociology.* New York: Columbia University Press, 1976.